M000307329

Presented To:

_____

From:

_____

Date:

_____

The
Counterfeit
Christian

The
Counterfeit
Christian

BEING AWARE OF THE ENEMY AND
KNOWING YOUR TRUE PURPOSE

LUIS LOPEZ

DESTINY IMAGE₀ PUBLISHERS, INC.
P.O. Box 310, Shippensburg, PA 17257-0310
"Promoting Inspired Lives."

This book and all other Destiny Image, Revival Press, MercyPlace, Fresh Bread, Destiny Image Fiction, and Treasure House books are available at Christian bookstores and distributors worldwide.

For a U.S. bookstore nearest you, call 1-800-722-6774.
For more information on foreign distributors, call 717-532-3040.
Reach us on the Internet: www.destinyimage.com.

ISBN 13 TP: 978-0-7684-3970-0
ISBN 13 Ebook 978-0-7684-8934-7

For Worldwide Distribution, Printed in the U.S.A.
1 2 3 4 5 6 7 8 / 15 14 13 12 11

Dedication

To my *Lord and Savior Jesus Christ*, You have made me realize after all these years what true love really is. Thank You so much, Lord God, for being who You are; I love You so much. You have helped me to know who I am and how to really love my wife, others, and myself. I am so thankful. When the world engulfed me with its thirst, You remained the Living Water that has always given me true drink. I sincerely thank You with all of who I am. And I thank You for the anointing to write this book for Your people. The closer I get to You, the more You overwhelm me. Thank You so much, Lord. You are so real!

To my wife, *Prophetess Michelle Lopez*, who has been with me from the beginning, dealing with the intense and elongated hours I have poured into this book. You are the love of my life and a powerful woman of God. You really are my best friend; I am so glad we met 20 years ago. My soul has a reason to live when I am with you. You have been with me through the tough, hard, good, and crazy times. Thank you so much for believing in me with this project and for helping me put it together. Your heart will always be part of mine! I am loving you to the very end of time.

To my mother, *Naomi Hernandez-Lopez*, I would not even be here if it weren't for you. You are everything to me; there are no words to describe how much I really, truly love you, Mom. I will never forget the love and the struggles you endured in dealing with me and believing in me. Thank you for your prayers. Thank you for the wisdom and guidance you poured into me when I needed you the most; I love you.

To the rest of my family, I thank God for each and every one of you. Love you all forever: *Josiah, Annamarie, Chelsea, Joel, Jose,* and *Dante.*

To *Dr. Keith Nesbitt, Sr.* Thank you, Sir, for the opportunity and the information you have poured into me throughout the years. My family and I appreciate all the good you have shown us; I assure you it has not been in vain. Truly, without you, this book would not have been possible. A million thanks. I love you, brother.

Acknowledgments

I would like to acknowledge a few new friends of mine and those who have been there since the beginning.

Julio E. Montalvo (Kre8tor)—I would like to thank you because you were the first one who led me to Christ back in 1987 when you spoke to me about the Book of Revelation while sitting on your dining room floor. It really scared me at first, after hearing you for a little while, before the eyes of my heart opened to receive understanding and afterward *no fear,* thank God! I will never forget that day when we walked into your mother's living room, when I stood in a circle hand-in-hand with your family, giving my life to Christ for the first time and feeling the Holy Spirit literally move in my spirit. That was an awesome experience! Thank you, Sir, for leading me to the Lord. I will always be grateful to you, Betsy, Michelle, Eddie Sr., and Eddie Jr. That was an amazing day for me. I will always love you no matter what; I consider you like my real brother.

Apostle Demond L. Holley and Elect-Lady Tenille Holley. I would like to thank you both for the kindness, hospitality, and sincerity that you have demonstrated to my wife and me. We appreciate you and love you both very much.

Evangelist Donna Johnson and family—my wife and I would like to thank you so much for being obedient to the voice of God and confirming what the Lord had spoken to us a few months earlier. I dedicate this book to you as well. You are loved and appreciated.

Pastor Dan Willis and Jason Grant (DJ Pookie), at TCT Christian Television Network, hosts of the "I'm Just Sayin" broadcast—I would like to extend many thanks to the entire network and television crew in Detroit, Michigan. Thank you all for your hospitality and the opportunity for us to be on your television program. Also I would like to acknowledge Dr. Garth and Tina Coonce. God bless you all.

Endorsements

Apostle L. Lopez, Jr. is an end-time apostle who has been given revelation knowledge and prophetic insight of the times. God has given him the ability to see through the eyes of the Lord. I recommend this book to the Body of believers. Apostle Lopez is a true man of God who has been given divine instructions for the Body of Christ today! His wisdom will open the eyes of your understanding by the anointing of the Holy Ghost. This manuscript will equip you for these end times so you will be well-prepared for all the enemy tries to accomplish in your life!

Lopez and his wife have been called in the Kingdom of God for such a time as this. The Lord is calling forth the apostles and the teachers in this hour to reveal how to damage the works of the devil effectively. I know this work he has written will help maneuver many to be in right standing in the Spirit. People need to be prepared in this season to become well-learned in the Scriptures. I am pleased to know him and his wife. I feel with the love of Christ in my heart, that they are "a Kingdom-minded ministry." *Judah House of Praise* and I are very blessed to be a part of this project. God bless you, Apostle and Prophetess Lopez.

APOSTLE AHMAD R. LEE
Judah House of Praise Int'l Word Ministries Church
Monroe, NC

This book is an easy read and a page-turner. I kept reading because, for a moment there, I thought Luis had peaked into the recesses of my mind and had begun to answer the many questions that I had about people. I have pastored for 12 years, but no one told me how the spirits would come against the Word of God, how people would carry these spirits from place to place, how people would even think they were not possessed, but that the spirit oppressed, suppressed, and depressed them by the spirit. This book has put the Word of God in such clarity for me. It is so simple; even a fool will not error. The Introduction reached out and grabbed my attention and drove me through the next few chapters eagerly. I pray that every newborn creature in Christ will read this book because it is a manual to prepare them to get on the battlefield for the Lord and not be distracted by the "counterfeit," but follow after the real things of God. May God richly bless you.

PASTOR THOMASINA T. OWENS
Morning Star Missionary Baptist Church
Rochester, NY

The first time I met Apostle Lopez, I saw the anointing in him, that God has ordained him to be a great warrior in this hour. Ever since I have known Brother Lopez, I found him to be sound in God and unmovable in his calling. I believe this book will be a life-changer for those who read it and examine it thoroughly.

EVANGELIST DONNA JOHNSON
Fountain of Joy Church
Pounding Mill, VA

Some will read a word inspired by God and give us what they have read, or they will be inspired by a message they have heard from some one else of influence and give us what they have gathered. But Apostle and Prophetess Lopez have been given a sound word for this hungry and desperate generation from the Spirit of God Himself. In this book, Apostle Lopez goes deeper than religion, tradition, or culture has ever gone before; with details of his experience and findings—he leads us. And he also leads the people of God out of compromise and complacency into a deeper place of relationship, and right fellowship with God. In this work, he exposes the enemy with simple truths and revelations. He achieves this with light and inspiration from above. The wisdom poured into this work is certainly from our Father. We trust that this is an international word that must be extended to everyone. We were destroyed due to lack of knowledge, but God sent a humble, kind, and compassionate servant by the name of Apostle Lopez, and we now live in truth!

BISHOP J.D. BROWN and PASTOR T. BROWN
Separated By Purpose Ministries
Rochester, NY

Apostle Luis Lopez is a profound author and teacher. Apostle Lopez's messages are ahead of his time. I would urge anyone to get a copy of this book, read it, and pass it

on. The Lopez's ministry has an anointing level that surpasses that of all people that called themselves apostles.
Apostle Luis Lopez is a modern-day John the Baptist.

PROPHET MATTHEW J. HENDRIX
Morning Star Missionary Baptist Church
Founder of Fresh Fire and Wind Ministries
Rochester, NY

I believe this book will show you your true self as you
take a look in the mirror to see who you are. Apostle Lopez
is very knowledgeable and consistent in his insight for the
true walk for the Christian. Honestly, as you read more of
these pages, I pray that it would convict you and turn you
from your ways and help you understand who you are and
understand the Bible more today.

APOSTLE MICHAEL E. THOMAS
4C.I.T. Ministries International
Chicago, IL

Contents

Foreword

I am very pleased to be able to write this foreword for this wonderful book. Apostle Lopez is one of the finest men of God I have had the pleasure of knowing and loving. The apostle's insight into the Word of God and his prophetic gifts can only have come from God Himself. Together with his lovely wife and children, they set the example for today's Christians and what we should strive for in our own walk with Christ. I'm sure you will grow to the next spiritual level simply by reading this wonderful book written by a wonderful man of God. I love you, my brother in Christ.

> *Therefore, my beloved brethren, be steadfast, immovable, always abounding in the work of the Lord, knowing that your labor is not in vain in the Lord* (1 Corinthians 15:58 NKJV).

Dr. Keith Nesbitt, Sr.
Faith Bible Theological Seminary

Introduction

The reason for writing this book is to prepare the Body of Christ for the coming Messiah. You must know who you are in Christ and what you are capable of doing for the Lord while you're here on earth. In order for you to achieve the blessings of God and be victorious, you must follow the path of obedience with humility. In my writings, you will read a lot about the heart, mind, and spirit to help keep you in alignment with the Word of God, positioning yourself to receive the blessings that have been waiting on you.

What you are about to read is going to equip, encourage, empower, edify, correct, instruct, build up, and prepare you to become aware of the enemy's strategies and devious counterfeits, which many times come in the form of people you encounter in your everyday living. You will know the true meaning of your life in Christ when you keep away from such a crowd. For too long the devil has uprooted and torn down many born-again believers into thinking they are worthless and cannot obtain their true function in life. You were created for more than just going through the motions and hoping that one day things will turn out for your good. Well, your day is *now!*

The enemy's agenda is to bring confusion, striking the weak and fainthearted with all he has, causing believers to lose their route, impeding them from becoming the very thing God has called them to be. In this book, I hope to assist believers in escaping a spirit of unwillingness and equip Christians who have faltered and forgotten who they really are, giving them the proper tools to reach their purpose. The adversary has determined to target and then assault those who are already in bondage. Therefore, carrying a canopy of blindness with him, he places it over the eyes of Christians to elude them from their promises and the unlimited blessings that God has already stored up for their lives.

Jesus Christ has commissioned me to be His "apostle to the nations," mandating my wife and me with the purpose and plan to bring true righteousness and holiness to the Body of believers in this nation and around the world, preparing them for Christ's imminent return. Like what John the Baptist did for Christ in the First Coming—he prepared the way for the Lord—I shall do for Christ's Second Coming, by His command. I must be obedient. And in my obedience, I pray that this book and the anointing of the Holy Ghost fall on you as you read, and when you are finished reading, may the presence of God flood you with His everlasting love, peace, and grace.

—Luis Lopez

CHAPTER ONE

Guard Your Heart and Spirit

Keep [guard] *thy heart with all diligence; for out of it are the issues of life.*

—PROVERBS 4:23

omparing the real to the counterfeit tells you a lot about the imitation. The sole purpose of the counterfeit is to fool people into thinking they have equal value to the original. But when we put both the counterfeit and the real into the light, it tends to reveal the original from the imitation. If the replicas do not have the eternal seal, the strip to prove their authenticity, God will cast them into the *lake of fire*, never to be received, heard, or seen again (see Rev. 20:15).

There are many believers who do not realize the infinite power that lies within the deepest part of who they really are. I pray that, as you read, your faith will be empowered, becoming sharper and more attentive to the enemy's devices; I pray too that you will come to know your definitive purpose in this life, whether it's through people, the supernatural, or both.

We must continue to believe God. Many have swayed from the Lord and believed life with Christ was not something to be part of. Christians who once were on fire for God have given up or, worse, have committed suicide. Countless others in the faith and in the world have been deceived. They have been lured away from the truth of God's Word by the so-called "good things" of this world, its system, and its beliefs. Tragically, these poor souls have given into false hopes, visions, and dreams that promise new life, lots of money, or certain freedoms; but in the end, these counterfeits only end up destroying people's lives, sometimes slowly, sometimes quickly.

The message I bring to you is reassurance, that the plan Christ has for you is greater than you can ever ask or think. I also want you to be aware of others who claim to be "saved and sanctified." They claim to be filled with the Holy Spirit, and some are filled truly, but they are engaged with a spirit that is not holy.

As a matter of fact, whether or not a person is truly saved and sanctified is a heart and spirit issue most of the time. Many concentrate on the mind, but the heart, the spirit, and the devil also need to be dealt with; otherwise we could find ourselves in unfathomable trouble. As we all know, there are many thoughts running around in the minds of believers. We must be scrupulous in how we confess those things into our environment, especially with other individuals inside and outside of our comfort zones.

DID YOU KNOW?

In college, I learned that the heart communicates with the brain through an inherent nervous system, which assists in making decisions and influences perception. The heart has a 40,000-neuron brain inside it, which can learn, sense, feel, and hold memory all by itself. This reminds me of what the Bible says, *"...Out of the abundance of the **heart**, the mouth speaketh"* (Matt. 12:34), *"For as he **thinketh** in his **heart**, so is he..."* (Prov. 23:7), and *"For where your treasure is, there will your **heart** be also"* (Matt. 6:21).

What we don't hear from the ear of our hearts, too often, is the fact two plans are available to humankind. God has a plan for our lives, and the devil also has a plan for our lives. One is for our destruction, and the other is for our good, unto life eternal. The lie of the devil is to steal our dreams, kill our relationships (engagements, marriages, friendships, business partnerships, and the like). It is true what the Sacred Text says about *our common* enemy, who goes to and fro throughout the earth to make sure no good comes to you (see Job 1:7; 1 Pet. 5:8). This is why we must always be prepared spiritually and naturally, making sure when we start our hand-to-hand combat, which is prayer, that we can go to war with assurance, boldness, and holiness in the power of the Holy Ghost.

If you have no prayer life with God, the enemy will mock you, and you will become an easy target. Remember, beloved, without a prayer life, your walk with Christ will be very short and will slowly fade and diminish. You have to pray every single day for the rest of your life. You cannot give up because satan is not giving up on you until you are gone from this life. He wants to make sure that God is nowhere to be found in your everyday thoughts.

Meditate on these passages:

> *The thief cometh not, but for to steal, and to kill, and to destroy...* (John 10:10).

> *For we wrestle not against flesh and blood, but against principalities, against powers, against the rulers of the darkness of this world, against spiritual wickedness in high places* (Ephesians 6:12).

> *(For the weapons of our warfare are not carnal, but mighty through God to the pulling down of strong holds;) casting down imaginations, and every high thing that exalteth itself against the knowledge of God, and bringing into captivity every thought to the obedience of Christ; and having in a readiness to revenge all disobedience, when your obedience is fulfilled* (2 Corinthians 10:4-6).

> *But if our gospel be hid, it is hid to them that are lost: in whom the god of this world hath blinded the minds of them, which believe not, lest the light of the glorious gospel of Christ, who is the image of God, should shine unto them* (2 Corinthians 4:3-4).

Here are several Scriptures you can pray to speak against the enemy and to guard your heart, mind, and spirit:

No weapon that is formed against thee shall prosper; and every tongue that shall rise against thee in judgment thou shalt condemn. This is the heritage of the servants of the Lord, and their righteousness is of Me, saith the Lord (Isaiah 54:17).

Have you an arm like God? Or can you thunder with a voice like His? (Job 40:9 NKJV)

He has shown strength with His arm; He has scattered the proud in the imagination of their hearts (Luke 1:51 NKJV).

...For the battle is not yours, but God's (2 chronicles 20:15 NKJV).

Your right hand, O Lord, has become glorious in power; Your right hand, O Lord, has dashed the enemy in pieces (Exodus 15:6 NKJV).

Finally, my brethren, be strong in the Lord and in the power of His might (Ephesians 6:10 NKJV).

The eternal God is your refuge, and underneath are the everlasting arms; He will thrust out the enemy from before you, and will say, "Destroy" (Deuteronomy 33:27 NKJV).

..."Not by might nor by power, but by My Spirit," says the Lord of hosts (Zechariah 4:6 NKJV).

DISCERN THE COUNTERFEITS

Counterfeit Christians come in all different forms. *Counterfeit* means "to imitate, to forge, to feign, and to simulate." In these last days, numerous people will admit to being on the side of God. These people may be relatives, followers of other religions, friends, or associates you highly respect. The apostle Paul, in First Corinthians 12, wrote about the nine gifts of the Holy Spirit, which will help us discern the specific spirits in people. The particular gift I'm going to mention is very important, just as the others—the gift of discernment of spirits. *Charismata* in Greek is translated as "power, authority gifts."[1] The Lord, by His Spirit, will establish these "power gifts" to His children as He wills.

It's very important to have this discernment, especially when we have individuals from all areas of life come into our circles. We cannot *always* have people touch us, pray for us, and give us words. We shouldn't always invite all different kinds of people into our homes, either. Not every voice that says, "I love Jesus" is right in the eyes of our God. The Scriptures state, *"Lay hands suddenly on no man..."* (1 Tim. 5:22 KJV). This is not to say we should make everyone we encounter feel uncomfortable and offended. But we should be discerning and aware of our surroundings—aware of who is surrounding us, like a watchmen or seers, a type of prophet according to the Bible. If we don't walk in the Spirit with discernment, we will be inviting all different kinds of spirits into our homes.

Demonic spirits are spiritual hitchhikers. They cling to the ignorant, and they follow, sleep, and hunt the weaker ones in the faith (see Hos. 4:6). If you think you do not have the gift of discerning of spirits, or if you do have it, but do not know how to use it, pray and ask the Lord for help. Also speak to the leaders of your church for guidance in this area. In the meantime, watch those you meet to see if their fruit is ripe and fresh. If you do not take this seriously, the outcome can be devastating; people without knowledge will start transferring spirits one to another. This is dangerous to the believer and the Church. Please be very careful as the days begin to engulf the world with evil.

GUARD YOUR SPIRIT

When you relate with believers or sinners, or when you are making home and hospital visits, pray and anoint yourself with oil if you do not know the people you are dealing with. Protect your spirit with the Word of God to make sure your spirit and mind do not wander into places they shouldn't. Guard your gates (ears, eyes, nose, and so forth), because it is not always easy to see when spirits try to attack you or attach themselves to you (thus the importance of discerning spirits). You must guard your gates because unclean spirits can enter through your nose and mouth, and when they are cast out, they come out where they entered.

Proverbs 4:7 declares, *"Wisdom is the principal thing, therefore get wisdom, and in all your getting, get understanding"* (NKJV). I mention this passage because we need the wisdom and understanding of God, and not people, in order to understand the realm of the Spirit. I am talking about things above and beyond human understanding and intellect. For example, certain diseases have no cure, and doctors cannot explain why. Some physical ailments are actually spiritual, but it boggles the human mind and is, therefore, categorized by doctors as unexplainable. This same reliance on human understanding causes people to be unaware that demons travel and follow people around in the spirit, harassing them. Sometimes this happens on a day-to-day and night-after-night basis, while people have no clue what is really going on with them, their household, or their children.

I hear statements like, "I don't know what it is about them or this house, but I feel uncomfortable" or "I feel like something bad is going to happen if I stay and don't leave." Sometimes we may become frustrated, feel angry, get headaches, feel sick all of a sudden, or spit up blood. This is a spirit of witchcraft, anger, a strong fence of warlockism, rebellion, and stubbornness that is coming against us.

Some people experience these things as they lack prayer—almost an inability to pray. They know they need to pray, when they feel the unction of the spirit, it's like they are being squeezed, and it affects their prayer lives. The slave girl, or "damsel," in the Book of Acts was named Alpithia. She had a spirit of divination called Python, or Apollo, which in Greek is *Pythian Apollo* (see Acts 16:16). This spirit of python slithers its way into Christians' and unbelievers' heads, wrapping itself with the objective of constricting and choking the Word of God and prayer out of their hearts and minds, causing them to be unfruitful and lacking. (We must come against it and fight back, keeping the Word with all that is within us, because the end is near.)

Now he who received seed among the thorns is he,
who hears the word, and the cares of this world

and the deceitfulness of riches choke the word, and he becomes unfruitful (Matthew 13:22 NKJV).

Now the ones that fell among thorns are those who, when they have heard, go out and are choked with cares, riches, and pleasures of life, and bring no fruit to maturity (Luke 8:14 NKJV).

In the days we live in, this python spirit is *one* of countless spirits that causes us to struggle to read God's Word and pray. When we are about to open up our Bibles and read, we may not know what to read, and we experience all sorts of interruptions coming in every direction. The baby cries, the kids start fighting, the phone rings, and so forth—disruption surrounds us all. This proves that there is a spiritual war that is beyond all of our imaginations combined, and it is happening in the supernatural realm. Unfortunately, a lot of believers do not believe in the spiritual realm, denying that hell or the devil even exist. Of course, God is more powerful than anything in existence (He is the Creator of all things), but we do not want to be ignorant of the fact that evil spirits exist.

CLEAN HOUSE

Demonic spirits occupy the first and second heaven, which is our atmosphere, as well as where the Sun, Moon, and Stars reside. For those who need guidance in order to realize what is necessary, who need help in their walk with Christ; I have listed some reasons why these attacks occur:

- Living in disobedience or partial obedience: which means an individual is not truly taking the Word of the Lord at its full potential seriously, and only obeying parts of it, or none at all.

- Unawareness/ignorance: It's no excuse not to be aware of God and His ways. You must become aware and disregard that ignorance is bliss.

- Participating in necromancy; contact with practicing mediums, sorcery, even speaking to the dead.

- Use of white and black magic (through witches and warlocks).

- Use of demonic video games, movies, certain television shows, and anything else that may welcome evil spirits to have entry in your life and home.

- Involvement in false religion, including idol figures, or figurines, even your worship of such things.

- Involvement with Santeria, witchcraft, Wicca, or Voodoo, whether it be out of curiosity or because friends have influenced you to dabble in it.

- Use of demonic books, statues, pictures/images, or Ouija boards.

- Generational curses, pride, or the spirit of leviathan, which is a stronger pride of haughtiness operating in and through your life.

- Familiar spirits: things which are recognized by family and friends that may have access in your life. Such as: mediums, witches, wizardry, sorcery, alcoholism, loose living, drugs, etc. (see Lev.19:31; Isa. 19:3).

- Desert spirits, animal spirits, or animal sacrifices (see Isa. 34:11-15).

- Refusal to believe that satan exists is one of the most popular in the secular world. Most believe the devil is a figment of our imagination. We must know that the Bible clearly states he and his fallen ones exist (see Rev. 12:9).

- Rejection of Jesus Christ as Lord and Savior is one main reason for multitudes to be cast out from God's presence (see John 3:3; Matt. 8:12).

- Interaction with spiritual birds or fowl allowed to enter into the arena of your inner circle can also be very dangerous. Guard your gates at all times so you will not be ensnared (see Eccl. 9:12).

CURSED OR NOT CURSED, THAT IS THE QUESTION

People are spirits having a physical experience. Many believers and people in the world think spirits are just in the mind, and they explain it away into unbelief. But now that you are aware of the things on the list, you should pray and seek out guidance. Someone in your church, like a pastor or minister, should set a date to visit your residence and begin the process of closing open portals, casting out all evil and unclean spirits, and anointing your home.

I knew some friends who were believers, but they were messing around with a Ouija board to see if it was real. They thought it was just fantasy, a game of make believe, but as time went by, they realized that it did work. Things don't just fall off the center of the table, touch your body, speak to you audibly, or float in the air all by themselves! In addition, more demonic activity invaded their home—devilish entities would speak to them, and terrible visions and other overwhelmingly evil activities tormented them. Ultimately, I discontinued from visiting their home and felt the need to educate myself to be aware of these unclean practices. I did feel bad for them, but being a young Christian, I had no idea what to say or how to handle such things. They wanted to be free from it, but I really didn't have a clue how to deal with supernatural issues like that one.

One thing I've learned studying about cults and the occult is that you *never* burn or discard a Ouija board where it can be seen; you throw it in a river or a deep pit where no one would find it. If you burn it, you will curse yourself, and you shouldn't give it away to someone else. Those spirits will fall on the person who finds it. These spirits are dangerous and life-threatening. Evil spirits do not dally with you at all; they play for keeps, and the prime objective is to have your soul in hell forever. In all seriousness, God does not have time to play around; time is running out! Many Christians who claim to know Him really just know *of* Him, and they do nothing He says. Certainly, millions of people have no idea what we are up against. The invisible realm is more powerful than we are in the natural. A friend told me a few years ago that His Professor in college, who was a Scientist, stated that in the 6th dimension we can eat an orange from the inside out. Imagine that!

REVELATION: THE ENEMY'S PLAN

This reminds me of a revelation the Lord showed me a few years ago that brought me to my knees. The Holy Spirit took me to the 11th dimension of the spirit realm, and I saw Jesus Christ sitting on His throne in Heaven. The Mighty God (see Isa. 9:6) sitting above the heavens and the earth was breathtaking and glorious!

Writing about Christ sitting on His throne in Heaven stirred my recollection of a program I watched about NASA, its scientists, and theory on physics. Astronomers and astrophysicists claim they have reached the end of the universe to the farthest northern point. Now, if you are familiar with numbers, you would find that if you were to stack a trillion dollars in one hundred dollar bills on top of each other, it would stand about 739 miles above the earth. Having that in mind, I recall one night as I was watching Jack Van Impe on television, he was stating that NASA has come to a phenomenal discovery, that the end of the universe is 187 trillion billions of miles; imagine that in one hundred dollar bills.

In conclusion, pertaining to my own personal research in over 55,000 hours of reading, hearing, and studying God's Word, I believe the Lord's Heaven is in the north, in the constellation "Swan," according to the Scriptures and astronomical studies (astrology is the perversion of astronomy). As I studied the Holy Text and sought the Lord with much prayer, I began to perceive what the enemy was conjuring up in his mind to come against the Lord. Satan and the fallen angels tried to take the Father's position with a military tactic to bring down the Creator from His throne in Heaven. He tried to outsmart God by flanking Him *"in the sides of the north"* (Isa. 14:13). Satan's plan failed, of course, confirming what Jesus said: *"I saw Satan fall like lightning from heaven"* (Luke 10:18 NKJV).

This is the revelation I have received from the Word, but I understand that not everyone will agree. I recognize the fact that Heaven is northward, but to say exactly where in the north is impossible; no one truly knows unless they are there.

> *For thou hast said in thine heart, I will ascend into heaven, I will exalt my throne above the stars of God: I will sit also upon the mount of the congregation,* **in the sides of the north** (Isaiah 14:13).

ALL JOKES ASIDE

Beloved, let's not take His Word as a joke. We need to get it together, to heed to what the Lord commands and stay away from the enemy's devices. One of the enemy's schemes, which is one of the most powerful deceptions, is to lead people into thinking he doesn't exist (see 1 Pet. 5:8). This is how he deceives us, causing us to think it's merely the person we are dealing with that is the problem, when there is much more influencing that individual.

A lot of religious people have a hard time following the Lord. My counsel to you is, if you are struggling in your walk with the Lord, contact a leader or your pastor immediately. Let that person guide you or assign someone into your life to help you in your journey with Christ. Allow the pastor to choose someone who could hold you accountable so that when you need help, it's accessible. Remember the words of the Bible; we must make sure we are doers of the Word and not hearers only, deceiving ourselves (see Jas. 1:22). We must follow His Word and do what He instructs us to do.

> *But why do you call Me "Lord, Lord," and do not do the things which I say?* (Luke 6:46 NKJV)

> *Hypocrites! Well did Isaiah prophesy about you, saying: "These people draw near to Me with their mouth, and honor Me with their lips, but their heart is far from Me. And in vain they worship Me..."* (Matthew 15:7-9 NKJV).

SPEAK DEATH

The vicissitudes of religion and its founders will never disprove who the God of the Bible is—the God of Abraham, Isaac, and Jacob, the only one true God. We have to remain in a place of holiness in order to be used by the Spirit of God, to implement righteousness to those walking in error and a different spirit. These counterfeit delusions of Scripture are close to the words of the Great Architect, but those who teach them take away from the Holy Bible to build their case. They become blind guides and heretics, not knowing they are blind and unable to see or grasp the light of the surefire Gospel of Christ.

You must relentlessly stay true to the Creator of your youth, weathering the storms of adversity and indifference. The world will mock you, even if you are a businessperson, professional, or churchgoer. The devil makes no adjustments for you. Whether people say, "Hosanna" or "Crucify," you must keep striving diligently on the narrow path that leads to life eternal (see Gal. 6:9).

We who are chosen need to pray, read, fast, and consecrate ourselves to make sure that we are hearing the voice of Heaven and obeying Him. It can be very difficult at times, but we need to stop confessing that it's too hard and that we can't do it. Perhaps, if we refuse to speak this way, our walk might just become a little easier. *"I can do all things through Christ who strengthens me"* (Phil. 4:13 NKJV).

The devil hears us and hangs on to every word that comes out of our mouths; we must make sure we do not become superfluous with our words. He is our antagonist, an adversary who tries to bring destruction with all kinds of circumstances to prevent us from going farther. We often quote combat verses, such as, *"speak life"* (Prov. 18:21) to resist negative conditions as we live our lives for God. Let me take it further; we need to also speak death! Speaking death to those things that should not be in our lives will start to improve our spiritual awareness. We will notice that breakthroughs will begin to explode, and we will possess a new fervor, setting us in motion in order to have sweet victories.

Speak death to that cancer! Speak death to all destructive relationships and soul ties (see Prov. 18:21). In God's eyes, it is very crucial for us to do His will. His plan is so much better than ours. Do His will at all costs! To God be all the glory and honor! The real question is, are we willing to pay the price? We must never give up on speaking life and death into our volatile situations; then we can watch how the Lord will turn it around for our good. *"Death and life are in the power of the tongue, and those who love it will eat its fruit"* (Prov. 18:21 NKJV).

IT'S NOT FAIR

There was a man who was terrible to a lot of people on our street, and this man had a son who went to the neighborhood school. Some of the boys in his class knew that he was that man's son. Every time he walked home from school, they would take their frustrations out on him and beat him up just because of his father's bad attitude.

It's not fair that the son had to pay for his father's behavior, but his story is a picture of life—we are judged for all kinds of things. We are judged for our appearance, the kinds of clothes we wear, the cars we drive, the people we love and speak too, and so forth. This is the heart of satan; he hates the fact that we look, talk, and sound like Jesus Christ. Satan, with all that he has in his arsenal, tries to stop us from speaking God's Word, especially through tough times. He is always on the prow to destroy us, trying to send all kinds of harm our way with no remorse in his heart (and believe me, he has no heart).

Christians sometimes don't have even a hint of how to handle his tactical approach, and they give up on God because the fire was too hot to bear. The trials are many and continuous, and as we well know, one trial will end just for another to rise up in its place. I was brought up with the saying, "Tough times don't last; tough people do." Many people become bitter and very angry because of all the unexplainable troubles they have had to endure. We must be careful how we exhibit our anger with others and particularly toward God. This might sound funny, but sometimes we have to forgive God, too.

It is sinful to retain an angry heart toward God and others. We are commanded by the Lord to love Him and our neighbors with all that we have in us (see Luke 10:27). I have found approximately 31 instances of "love one another" in the Scriptures. No matter what kind of a neighbor people are to us, or others, we must learn to love them as ourselves (this is not always easy to do). As time goes on and as we get closer to God, He gives us the grace to pursue and follow His commandments. It is difficult to live a life of total humility, always determined to pursue the spirit and not get offended with others or say and do things we shouldn't.

When I had the privilege of meeting a well-known author, speaker, and anointed man of God, Mike Murdock in Buffalo, New York, several years ago, he told me one thing that I will never forget. First he gave my wife and me a word for our children, and then he spoke a word to me personally, which changed my whole way of thinking about my walk with Christ. It was such a simple word, but it meant the world to me at that time. Ever since he spoke that word to me, I always kept it in the back of my mind. I was going through a lot of issues with my family then, and that one small word just stood out, and I would repeat it and keep it in my prayers.

I have learned that a word from God in season will build you up, and a word out of season will do more harm then good. We must be sensitive and obedient when He speaks through His anointed ministers, and we must also learn to heed His still small voice in our prayer closets. This way we can learn when to speak the word and when to retain it as we go forth.

ARE WE ALL CHILDREN OF GOD?

The Scriptures state that the world does not know us because they didn't know Jesus, either (see 1 Cor. 2:14; 1 John 4:5; and Luke 24:16). Thus, they really don't recognize who we are because they are spiritually dead and their ears are stopped—this verse is still true to this day. When speaking about God and His children, the Bible always uses a symbol of intimacy and relationship, like that of a parent to a child (see Matt. 18:4). He would not separate His children from Himself or put us into obscure categories. Instead, He encourages His children to walk in the admiration of reading His Word, spending time with Him, loving Him, and ministering His Word to others. But unbelievers do not have any desire to give their lives just yet to the Lord, even though they know in their heart of hearts that they need to. Some are deceived, and this is when prayer comes in.

A particular young man said to me one day after service, as we were conversing about religious matters, "Why should I go to church when it's full of hypocrites?"

I replied, "That is cool how you are able to discern something so negative like that; if you give your life to Christ, you can demonstrate how not to become a hypocrite and lead them by example."

The young man stayed quiet for a moment, thinking about it, knowing he had at one time or another been a hypocrite himself. This is not to condemn anyone, but to cause people to think. Winning an argument is easy sometimes, but it's not worth losing the relationship. Speaking the truth with love and gentleness in humility is the key. In actuality, we are told to continuously attend church services; we are to assemble ourselves accordingly:

> *Not forsaking the assembling of ourselves together, as is the manner of some, but exhorting one another, and so much the more as you see the Day approaching* (Hebrews 10:25 NKJV).

One aspect of being a true child of God and not a hypocrite is being watchful for the return of Christ:

> *But ye, brethren, are not in darkness, that that day should overtake you as a thief. Ye are all the children of light, and the children of the day: we are not of the night, nor of darkness* (1 Thessalonians 5:4-5).

> *Behold what manner of love the Father hath bestowed upon us, that we should be called*

children of God; and such we are. For this cause
the world knoweth us not, because it knew Him
not. Beloved, now are we children of God, and
it is not yet made manifest what we shall be. We
know that, if He shall be manifested, we shall
be like Him; for we shall see Him even as He is
(1 John 3:1-2 ASV).

The verses above state that those who are not children and do not watch for Christ's return are in darkness—unaware of His coming and understanding. We who are saved are in the light and will watch for His coming.

We are described as a peculiar people, a holy nation that looks forward to Christ's second coming (see 1 Thess. 4:16, 17). The "second coming" is *invisible*; His "third coming" will be *visible* at the end of the seven-year tribulation period. Theologically, the *rapture* is not popularly known as the "second coming"; however, so we can understand it as a whole, in total doctrine it is true, and the rapture which is "invisible" will not fall along the lines as dogma, for the reason it is proven by the Word of God. To be clear in where I stand regarding the *catching away* of God's people, I believe that the "rapture" of the Church is a literal event to take believers into Heaven for judgment first, and then after seven years have gone by we come back to earth with our Messiah.

This is not a license to condemn, judge, or give up on people; God forbid! Regardless of whether they are children of God or not—whether they believe in the rapture, or whether they embrace post-tribulation or mid–tribulation belief—we must intercede and speak those things that are not as though they were (see Rom. 4:17). We must guide those who are not strong in the Lord to edify those who are not spiritually mature in God's Holy Word.

We must have an understanding, especially toward our own loved ones with much passion, commitment, and constant prayer, no matter who they are or what they've become—family, friends, or even our enemies. It's all about souls and love, loving people into the knowledge of God and the Kingdom of our Lord Jesus Christ and His Spirit, for the rejoicing of His Father. Proverbs 11:30 says, *"The fruit of the righteous is a tree of life, and **he who wins souls is wise**"* (NKJV). The apostle James further stated, *"Let him know, that he, which converted the sinner from the error of his way, **shall save a soul from death**, and shall hide a multitude of sins"* (James 5:20).

Speaking of rejoicing, for over three decades I was taught that it was the angels who would rejoice over a sinner who repents and comes to God. When we read Luke 15:10 carefully, however, we see it distinctively says, *"...There is joy in the presence of the angels of God over one sinner that repenteth."* This means that Jesus and the Father are throwing a party, and most likely, saints who have passed on are also joining in. Praise God!

I am so glad that the blood of Christ has cleansed us from sin, guilt, shame, and the stains of our past, giving us countless reasons to read and obey the Word of the Lord. He wants a real relationship with His children, with no hatred, bitterness, or sinful hearts lurking in our members. He wants us to love each other and to live peaceful lives. *"Blessed are the peace makers, for they shall be called the children of God"* (Matt. 5:9). God has a big plan for all His children, if we will only heed His voice. He is the only one who brings life, supporting us in all areas of our lives so that we can function and become more like Him every day.

The Lord said to me one day, "I resurrect death. I refresh what is stagnated. I am all that you need." That simply blew my mind. At that time, I needed to hear those exact words. He is always taking care of His own. No one can say that I do not hear His voice or that you are not capable of hearing His voice either. You belong to Him, and He belongs to you. God's children are those who are born again. *Sons* and *daughters* refer to the spiritually mature, but we are all His born-again children as long as we stay obedient to Him and His will. Not according to the abiding of the Law, but rather grace. Simply because we love Him enough to walk in obedience so His will may be accomplished in us.

Others outside of this understanding are His creation, and God does love them as well, but for them to earn the title of "Child of God" and enter Heaven, they must be redeemed (see John 3:3). We must come from the darkness into the light, which is Christ. This is not popular coming from the pulpit or certain books, but this is biblical. Many of us have tried everything by our own influence and in the power of the Holy Ghost to be holy and obedient to God. Nevertheless, we must remain open in a state of surrender from our wills for genuine liberation to visit and remain. We must keep that in mind every day for the rest of our lives. Being a Christian is a lifestyle and relationship, not a religion.

Jesus Christ is still the same yesterday, today, and forever all at the same time (see Heb. 13:8). Even God called Jesus, God, in the New Testament, confirming the status of His Son's position, validating who He was to give us strength to continue onward.

*But to the Son He says: "Your throne, O God, is forever and ever; a scepter of righteousness is the scepter of Your Kingdom. You have loved righteousness and hated lawlessness; **therefore God, Your God**, has anointed You with the oil of gladness more than Your companions"* (Hebrews 1:8-9 NKJV).

I know it's comforting and popular to call our loved ones children of God, but according to Scripture, if they have not truly accepted Jesus as Lord, they are not children of God. Not everyone who professes Christ or calls themselves Christians is in right standing with God. When we keep plugging these words into people's minds who do not have Christ the hope of glory living in their hearts, the enemy tends to deceive them into thinking they are God's children. This is how the devil distorts their minds so he can keep them from receiving Jesus as their personal Lord and Savior.

I have heard many preachers' kids who say, "Well Apostle Lopez, I am a child of God, and I go to church every Sunday faithfully, so I know I'm OK." In this scenario, they claim that, because their parents are church leaders, they have free access to God's Heaven. This is never true, and it's sad to say, in certain instances, such ones are worse than sinners. The devil has a main target on his mind, and it's to subtract anything associated with us and the Lord's promises for us. He lied to these preacher's kids I met, deceiving them like never before, and such deceptions are getting worse as the *day* approaches.

It makes no difference to him who we are or what church we belong to; he doesn't wait until we are filled with

God's Word and the Holy Ghost and then attack us. He starts his all-out assault when we are young and ignorant at a very early age. Notice, we never have to teach children how to be bad and selfish; they already know how, and we have to teach them how to be good and giving.

I have family whom I hold dear in my heart who think the same way—because their parents go to church, they believe they are OK. It hurts me when I think about how they live, since I want nothing more than for all of my extended family to be saved. In reality, it's up to them to choose, and I pray that they will choose life soon, before it's too late.

This has been a major issue. When I ask, "Where will you go if you died right now?" some have said, "To Heaven," many replied, "To the ground to rot," and others said, "I'm not sure." This kind of basic question gives men and women something to think about after I witness to them. This is where evangelism steps in. Not everyone who are called can evangelize and lead people into the Kingdom, it takes time and training. We have to be equipped and prepared for what's ahead of us. Jesus declared that it's the "gift and anointing" that He imparts for the believer to have the power to lead humans to salvation (see 2 Tim. 3:16, 17). We don't choose; He does the choosing and appoints us to go and bear fruit (see John 15:16).

NO LIMITS

Christians are the only ones who do not have to work their way into Heaven—unlike the followers of false religions and false gods, who believe in some sort of salvation through works. I am not saying that we shouldn't work; our faith without any works is dead, and works without faith is also dead (see James 2:17, 18). The Bible says whatsoever is not of faith is sin (see Rom. 14:23). My conclusion is that we don't have to work so hard trying to make it into Heaven; the price has been paid already through Jesus' death on the cross. I thought to myself the other day, *"How did Jesus pay a high price when He is God in the flesh, and when He died, He was able to pick His life up again?"* As soon as that thought entered into my head, the Holy Spirit said, "Son, I did pay a high price. I have given up My home and have taken on the form of *man*, for the rest of eternity."

In other words, Jesus ceased from transforming like He used to. I immediately understood what He was saying to me. In the Old Testament, Jesus would manifest Himself as all sorts of things—a burning bush (see Exod. 3:2), a pillar of cloud by day and fire by night (see Exod. 13:21), a Commander of the army of the Lord of Hosts (see Josh. 5:14, 15), and one of the three visitors entering into Abraham's tent (see Gen. 18:1-3). Now, Jesus is 100 percent Man as well as 100 percent God. He told His disciples, *"It's better for you if I leave, so the Father can send the Holy Spirit* [comforter]" (John 16:7). This happened so that Jesus the Lord could be around the world at the same time by bringing His Spirit to our planet. Jesus can do whatever He wants when He wants to do something that glorifies Himself and His Father. Limiting God would be foolish; He is sovereign.

My prayer to the Lord for you is that God would help you succeed in all that you do according to His will. In addition, I pray that you would never put limits in what He can do or has done. Unlimited is His name—*God*.

TWO FATHERS

There are two fathers who exist in our world today, the one in Heaven and the one here on earth. Father God and the father of lies (as we know, one is real, and the other is a counterfeit). We must bear the fruit of the Holy Spirit in order to differentiate who is who in these last days.

Aren't you blessed that you and I decided to choose God over the devil? This is a blessing beyond human comprehension. I feel a burden and deep concern thinking about loved ones, longing for them to make a decision to accept Christ as their Lord and Savior as I have done. Do not allow yourself to be deceived by the devil and his lies regarding you, and do not believe the lie that it is too late for your family to come to the Lord. Always pray for all of them and others to come to Christ, and pray that you would be equipped as you work out your salvation with fear and trembling (see Phil. 2:12; Ps. 2:11).

ATTIRE OF WAR

Make sure you put on the whole armor of God. If you do not, the enemy will have a soccer game in your mind. He doesn't play fair; he will make sure you will be open in your spirit for all different kinds of afflictions. As soon as you go to your place of employment, it will not take long before the devil shows his face. Here are some tips to help you confess and realize what this armor does for you. The Spirit of God recorded this for a purpose, to help you learn His ways of wisdom.

1. *Helmet of Salvation*—this protects your mind from the fiery darts of the enemy. Plead the blood of Jesus over your mind (soul), and pray for the helmet of salvation to protect your spirit. The soul and spirit are knit closely together. Remember, your soul needs to be renewed; your spirit is already saved and becomes a new creation in Christ Jesus. Romans 12:2 says that your soul—which is your mind—must be transformed, not your spirit. If you mix the two, it can lead to confusion, and God is not the author of disorder (see 1 Cor. 14:33, 40).

2. *Breastplate of Righteousness*—this piece of armor protects your heart. The Word states that people have desperate and immoral hearts (see Jer. 17:9). God is always looking and examining people's hearts. You must make sure that your heart is protected at all times. It's very important that you do not have unforgiveness or bitterness toward anyone. This can be a *huge* hindrance in your walk with Christ. Guard your heart, and most of all, forgive everyone (see Prov. 4:23).

3. *Shield of Faith*—this will protect you when hell's agents come your way with a different Gospel message. Make sure you are walking in your faith. Your faith will please God and will help you overcome the enemy's devices and become acquainted with your exact

purpose. Without *stubborn faith* in Christ, you will leave the Lord and go back to your old ways. Jesus said that if you leave your faith in God for another, even if it's your own, eight demons will enter into you, and the last state of your life will be worse than the first (see Matt. 12:43-45). Be a watchman, knowing that most times believing has a beginning and an ending; faith always is. I will talk more about that later.

4. *Belt of Truth*—this is similar to the Shield of Faith. Jesus is the truth. As long as He remains wrapped around your waist in the center of your body, you will always retain truth from within the depths of your spirit. Realize that belts have different levels; so does the truth of His Word. Christians go from glory to glory, faith to faith, and strength to strength.

5. *Sword of the Spirit* (the Word)—the spoken Word will always rebuke, expel, resist, banish, and destroy the works of the devil. Satan has no place to hide when you speak the eternal Word. The adversary hates it with a passion. A few Christians told me that demons would come and put their hands over their mouths as they were being attacked so that they were unable to say the name Jesus. Jesus *is* the Word. Demons know that the best way to assail believers is by first covering their mouths. The Word cuts both ways,

like a two-edged sword (see Heb. 4:12); be prepared always, and read your Word on a day-to-day basis.

6. *Gospel Shoes of Peace*—the steps of a good man are ordered by the Lord, and He delights in his ways (see Ps. 37:23). This piece of armor helps you know where you should and shouldn't go. When the enemy comes against you and begins to bring chaos into your dwelling, you know how to step on him and bruise his head! He is always going to be under your feet forever! He has no future, but you do.

TRIALS AND TESTS

As we know already, tests will come, and that is a promise from the Lord. So we must let our tests become our "test-imonies." There are 10,000 promises of God in the entire Bible—3,000 in the Old Testament and 7,000 in the New Testament. The Scriptures are filled with promises to build us up. These promises are not all for our good. Some of these promises have consequences that pertain to breaking the law and bringing death to our doorsteps. Now that I have become wiser, I ask God for His good promises. Allowing the text of His promises to reverberate from my mouth into the atmosphere of my home creates an environment of tranquility and hope. When we begin to act upon what He has already given us, we will see a variation in our attitudes, particularly when trials come our way.

It's a sad thing when people start out good with the Lord and then stop when the trials and tests of every day life come their way. When their faith is challenged, it causes some Christians to lose heart, keeping them from calling out to Jesus for help when they need to. We are nothing without Him. This is one thing the enemy used against me when I was a teenager. I allowed the devil for years to come and make me feel like such a hypocrite in the faith; I thought, *Why continue? You call yourself a Christian, and this is how you talk and act?* Once we tell people we are Christians, all eyes are on us. As if being attacked in the spirit wasn't enough, now here come hell's agents and counterfeit Christians ready to devour us in the natural. This used to knock me down and discourage me like nothing else.

As time went on, I became hungry and started to thirst for His righteousness once more. When satan tried again, bombarding my thoughts with doubt and unbelief, I fought back with the written Word, just like Jesus did in the desert, knowing that satan accuses and slanders. Stop him at his word, for only satan's words fall to the ground and will never stand against the Lord.

> *...The seed is the word of God. Those by the wayside are the ones who hear; then the devil comes and takes away the word out of their hearts, lest they should believe and be saved. But the ones on the rock are those who, when they hear, receive the word with joy; and these have no root, who believe for a while and in time of temptation fall away. Now the ones that fell among thorns are those who, when they have heard, go out and are choked with cares, riches, and pleasures of life, and*

bring no fruit to maturity. But the ones that fell on the good ground are those who, having heard the word with a noble and good heart, keep it and bear fruit with patience (Luke 8:11-15 NKJV).

THE CALL OF GOD

The Lord reminded me and said, "Son, I knew you were going to sin in the future, and I chose to save you anyway. I have forgiven you for the sins you did in the past and present and the sins you will commit in the future. They are all washed in My blood." (See First John 1:9.) My face lit up like a Christmas tree; that statement brought so much freedom into my life! I was a kid who was struggling, fighting to keep my faith. I was holding on to Jesus as if my life depended on it, and literally my life did depend on it. Through everything I have gone through, as I was hanging on, the Holy Ghost was the only one there for me.

Sure, I had the pastor and his leaders in my church to guide and teach me, but for some odd reason, it was like I was invisible to certain people. The feeling was like the Lord was keeping me from being involved in certain situations, keeping me on the side for something greater in my life. Even though these weird feelings and thoughts were running in the back of my mind, I would ignore them and try to get involved in some type of helps ministry. So I asked the pastor if I could be involved in the food ministry. The following week, one of the deacons came and allowed me to serve food for the homeless. Personally, I was happy the Lord used me to be a blessing to those in need. I made lots of friends while I was engaged in that ministry, and I loved it.

At the same time, having constant feelings that I couldn't be around people on an everyday basis drove me crazy. The Lord would separate me from friends, other Christians, and family. I didn't understand certain events and difficulties I had to go through as a teenager, particularly when confusion about what God was doing to me came in and out of my mind. Later on, as I continued walking with Christ and the ministers He would divinely set in my path, the Lord began to give me understanding of who I am.

Now I understand my call and that the trials that came my way were all for my good. Not everyone is called to be an apostle, prophet, evangelist, pastor, or teacher. That's not to say that no one has gone through something similar or worse than what I experienced. But when you are a teenager—full of energy, zealous, unlearned, wanting to hang out, eating everything in the fridge like a starving lion—you want to be around friends and have the great feeling that you are appreciated and important. It took time to understand the call that God had for me. Now without a shadow of any doubt, I know my call. Many didn't understand, and others still don't; that's OK. It's not my job to convince anyone. There were times when I just felt like giving up, but I knew I had to hold on to the call by hanging on with the strength He has given me. *"Now unto Him that is able to keep you from falling, and to present you faultless before the presence of His glory with exceeding joy"* (Jude 24).

LIFE LESSONS

To tell the truth, as the years went on, it took everything inside me, every fiber of my being, to hold on to Jesus. Trial after trial came my way constantly and didn't let up. Day after day, night after night, I was yelling out to Jesus to come and rescue me with tears streaming down my face. My father taught me a long time ago with his philosophy, saying, "Put your belt on tight son; men are not supposed to cry!" It took a long time to get that kind of thinking out of my head. For some reason (I know it's the Lord), I really didn't believe that. I would whisper to myself and say, "I am not a robot without feelings dad; a real man cries, a real man shows emotions, and a real man serves God!" Not allowing that deadly spirit of pride to control how I feel and think helped me in my walk with Christ. If I hadn't gone through my brokenness period, I wouldn't be married as long as I have been now. Just ask my wife.

Trials, anguish, and tests came and caused me to be on my face before God, calling out His name and asking Him to help me. I kept hearing thoughts in my mind, *You're not saved. What you feel isn't real; it's all in your head.* I'm sure we have all heard these thoughts at one time or another at work, school, church, or home. The enemy is opening fire and disrupting our thought processes with blazing darts into our minds, trying to get us off the narrow path. But the devil cannot physically take us off this path of life. He is only trying to prevent us from damaging his kingdom, trying to get us to fall away from Christ, utilizing every arsenal he has to make sure he prevails against us.

I believe we cannot lose our salvation, but we can give it up, and that is a slow fade. Imagine waking up one morning and telling someone, "Oh my goodness, I just lost my salvation!" Personally, I don't agree with that statement on the basis that it is never once found in Scripture. The Word of God tells us to work out our salvation with trembling and with fear (see Phil. 2:12), because repeated sinful behavior will lead people to backslide from God (but not just lose their salvation; I cannot perceive that happening).

We must stay strong in the Lord and in the influence of His strength. We cannot go on acting like we are high and mighty and holier than anyone else; we will lose potential souls instead of winning them for the Lord. We have to be very meticulous and cautious, learning to choose our words wisely at all times. Proverbs 10:19 tells us, *"In the multitude of words, sin is not absent."* This verse and most of the righteous and moral values found in Proverbs start in the home, learning to become examples one to another with a clear conscience, lifting our hands without wrath or doubting.

Since we can't just lose our salvation, if we are continually sinning, we will lose through physical death. The Bible says that after sin is complete it brings forth death (see Jas. 1:15). I am reminded of Samson when he kept playing around with sin and Delilah; eventually it all ended up short for Samson. He became prideful, thinking he had power of his own accord until the Philistines (who are now called Palestinians) came upon him. Clueless to the idea that the Lord would ever leave and abandon him, Samson was forsaken; the Philistines chained and severely punished him, including plucking his eyes out.

Those who revile God and His anointed (as you have just read concerning Samson) will end up in a place they cannot come back from. The Bible clearly states, *"Do not touch My anointed ones, and do My prophets no harm"* (1 Chron. 16:22; Ps. 105:15 NKJV). When we read the Book of Judges, we see that Samson kept lying to Delilah about where his strength came from until he ended up telling her the truth. He did not know that the Spirit of the Lord had left him. In the meantime, he kept telling her all different kinds of stories about where his strength came from. In one instance, he said to Delilah, "If you tie me up with this kind of rope then I will lose my strength." In his insolence and arrogance, claiming that his power came from his own authority, he lost it and became like any other man. Evidently, Samson was highly persuaded by evil desire and finally revealed to Delilah the secret about his hair. This was a very hard "life lesson" for Samson. (See Judges 16:1-31.)

Friends, we must not play with "Delilah," but stay far away from a spirit that will manipulate us like Delilah did to Samson is the best thing we can do. It gives a great meaning for the old saying, "If you play with fire, you will get burned." No matter the cost, we must always guard our hearts and our spirits!

PRAYER

Father, I believe you can do all things. I pray that you will continue to protect me from spirits that I am not aware of that try to cause me harm. I ask you God that I may remain in a place to be able to discern before I speak so I don't hurt your people or speak evil against them. Help me be one of the ones who demonstrate on a daily basis love, mercy, and compassion toward people that love you, and those who do not love you. My Lord, you said for us to ask for wisdom when we need it. My prayer will always be that You grant me wisdom for situations that have no light at the end, but that You will always be there for me as I continue to grow in you. Maturing always before your presence and respecting those who walk with Your authority. May I be humble the rest of my days. Holy Spirit continue to give me a clean heart before the Father, so blessings can overtake me and my family. I thank you Father for hearing my prayer. Thank you for loving me when there were times I couldn't even love myself. In Jesus' name I pray, Amen.

ENDNOTE

1.   www.thefreedictionary.com/charismata....s.v. "Charismata."

CHAPTER TWO

The Valley of Brokenness

*The Lord is near to those who have a broken
heart, and saves such as have a contrite spirit.*
—PSALM 34:18 NKJV

Teaching on the Valley of Brokenness is desperately
needed in the Body of Christ today. Multitudes of
saints have fallen off the path of life. Whenever my wife
and I minister to and mentor other couples and singles
whom God places in our path, the subject of brokenness
and humility always comes up. Their countenances fall and
they become fearful when I tell them that brokenness is
necessary in the heart of *every* Christian. On numerous
occasions, we have seen a change in their spirits that takes
them to an unusual level of disappointment. I explain to
them that God will be hindered if we do not embrace the
Valley of Brokenness simply because He does not use prideful and arrogant people.

When we are walking in the cloud of pride, it will cause destruction to ourselves and others around us. If we were to put one individual who has pride, secret sin, or a spirit of lying on the 21st floor of an office building and another one on the 2nd floor, they eventually would find each other. These prideful, sinful, and lying spirits will come into contact and connect one to another some way or another. Pride goes before destruction, the Bible tells us (see Prov. 16:18). This is why we need the Holy Spirit to change us; when we need to cry out to God and plead the blood of Jesus in order to be better in our circumstances and lives, He will hear us, especially in our most hurtful and desperate times of trouble.

Ironically, when change begins with its cousin *Mr. Uncomfortable*, we start to rebuke and destroy the works of the enemy. Really God is doing it—honoring our prayers from the night before, asking Him to change us and our ways. I have come to this conclusion; many of us really don't want to change for the better. Being comfortable is comfortable, and many of us do not want anything or anyone to remove us from our comfort zone. My inquiry is, how will God be able to do all these wonderful things for us and through us if we don't want to pay the price? Are we willing to pay the cost, or will we refuse to become broken? One reason why many get fearful is because the process of becoming broken really hurts. It's better for us to humble ourselves than for God to do it (see Jas. 4:10; 1 Peter 5:6). When God does it, it results in suffering. Humiliation is part of humility.

As I said in the previous chapter, love is humble. Love never fails, and it covers a multitude of sins (see 1 Peter 4:8). Prayer is very important in our lives. God loves us more than words can ever demonstrate. It will take eternity for God to show us how much He loves us, which is why we have to live in a body that never dies or gets old. Since God is eternal and His love is eternal, it's going to take eternity to show us His charity. His capacity to love is greater than ours, and His capacity to hurt is greater than ours. We have to submit and be humble in the sight of our God.

If we ask for brokenness in prayer, instead of allowing the Lord to do it, it will go well with us. Here are some passages that highlight the importance of humility:

> *Humble yourselves therefore under the mighty hand of God, that He may exalt you in due time* (1 Peter 5:6).

> *Humble yourselves in the sight of the Lord, and He will lift you up* (James 4:10 NKJV).

> *For whosoever exalteth himself shall be abased; and he that humbleth himself shall be exalted* (Luke 14:11).

> *The eyes of the Lord are on the righteous; and His ears are open to their cry. The face of the Lord is against those who do evil, to cut off the remembrance of them from the earth. The righteous cry out, and the Lord hears, and delivers them out of all their troubles. The Lord is near to those who have a broken heart, and saves such as have a contrite spirit. Many are the afflictions of the righteous, but the Lord delivers him out of them all* (Psalm 34:15-19 NKJV).

CONSECRATE ME, MY LORD AND MY GOD

Consecration isn't spoken about much from the pulpit these days. The word *consecrate* means, to make pure, holy, consecrate, set apart, devoting oneself to God, to regard as sanctification. This is when we separate ourselves from the noise, devoting ourselves to God completely with our time, looking to see what God's will is for our lives. No whining and complaining about how lonely we are or how we need to be around people—this is between just us and the Spirit, walking in total subjection to His will and plan.

We must come to God with humble hearts on a day-to-day basis. This is how we conquer the enemy. This is how we are able to meditate on His Word. This is how we become obedient and willing. If we do not humble ourselves and become broken, so He can pour out His anointing through us on an internal level, He will expose us and break us on an external level. That love process will be very painful and humiliating at times, but rewarding when it is over.

Men and women who are specifically and specially commissioned will not have the luxury of fitting in with the world at great levels. There will be instances when people won't understand us if they do not have an equal relationship with the Father as we do. Others may misrepresent us. Some may oppose us, and we will find ourselves lonely many times. We will be the ones always looking for friends to hang out with, but they will not be looking for us. God moves in stillness and in the quiet. Isaiah the prophet said that in quietness and in confidence will be our strength (see Isa. 30:15). Learning to be still will help us know that He is God.

When we are in spiritual training as ambassadors of Christ, we will need to have ears to hear what the Spirit is saying to *us*. There is no second-hand faith; we have to do this all alone, just us and the Holy Spirit. He will always point us to Jesus. As we remain in the quiet, we will start feeling a draw to spend more time with Him. In the wee hours of the morning, when He wakes us up to speak to Him and listen for His response, it will increase us in the Spirit. I believe The Word of God is placed *on* our hearts, (see Psalm 37:31), because after He begins to break us, His Word will fall right in without needing to force an entrance.

The Holy Spirit is a gentleman. He does not force Himself on anyone. All we have to do is make sure we are right in the sight of the Lord by doing what He commands. We must love Him with everything we are, calling out His name in the good times and the bad times. Turmoil doesn't always have to be our last name. Jesus' name is above everything imaginable in all of creation.

We have music, lyrics, artistry, dance, and so much more that demonstrates our love to Him and for Him. When we get close to the Lord and we begin to have a deeper relationship with Him, we will learn when to speak and when not to speak. After we do all the worshiping and praising of the Lord, we need to set an environment to have quietness and stillness rule in our homes. Learning to wait on the Lord in the quiet helps us to endure through hardships and troubles. The Bible says, *"It is good that a man should both hope and quietly wait for the salvation of the Lord"* (Lam. 3:26), and *"Be still, and know that I am God"* (Ps. 46:10 NKJV). Educating ourselves and building our character enables us to be able to listen, slow to speak, and slow to become angry when challenging issues arrive (see James 1:19).

BROKEN, BUT BLESSED

Broken, according to *Webster's Dictionary,* means, to be fractured, upheld, discontinuous, or interrupted. In a way this is true with God; when He decides to break us, we become fractured, broken, and interrupted in our everyday ways. We will see situations—which we were looking forward to having fall into place—suddenly discontinued. Things will become dry, and people start falling away from us. Slowly, but surely, it *will* happen. Sometimes, it will not even come through us asking. When the Lord chooses to interrupt us, it will come to pass. However, this mainly happens when God is calling us or training us for ministry.

We must always be in a place where we are able to listen to His voice while sensing His heart's desire for our lives. He is not a toy we play with any time we become bored and uninterested. Many unbelievers in the past have tested Him and have paid a high price. The owner of the Titanic stood on the bow, cursed God, and shook his fist to Heaven in doubt and anger, dictating to the Lord that He couldn't sink his ship. As you very well know, on the night of April 1912, a huge iceberg struck the ship and sank it,—as many have done in the past and still today.

For years, Christians have claimed they want to change their lifestyles, ways, or attitudes, but one thing they failed to realize is that if they haven't changed after all this time, as He has been pricking their hearts to change, it shows that they are not willing to go through the fire of brokenness. Like I always say, we must fall on the Rock and become broken, rather than having the Rock fall on us, causing us to become like ashes and dust. We have to learn to trust God with all our hearts; He knows how to change us and mold us. Fear is not of God. *"For God has not given us a spirit of fear, but of power and of love and of a sound mind"* (2 Tim. 1:7 NKJV). We must not let the devil stop us from becoming broken and poured out before God and other people. The Book of Psalms will help us to have a relationship with God by worshiping and praising Him correctly, and the Book of Proverbs will help us to have the wisdom to deal with other people.

The Holy Spirit is the Spirit of Christ. Christ came back to the earth and said, "A spirit doesn't have flesh and bone like I have" (see Luke 24:39). Where is His Spirit? He only mentioned that He was flesh and bone. The simple answer was that His Spirit is on the earth residing with us. This is a mystery, because the Bible says that Jesus' Spirit is not in Heaven, but in us (see Col. 1:27). Plainly, this means He is body and bone, but not Spirit, since He sent His Spirit here.

The Lord one day told me that He brought Jesus to the earth to show us He can be on the earth and in Heaven at the same time. (Of course, the purpose of Him coming to die was to redeem humankind, blameless and without sin, back to our Father.) This shows us that God is capable of doing whatever He wants whenever He wants. To know that God is omniscient, omnipresent, and omnipotent is a humbling thought.

On the other hand, we never need to feel afraid, but to embrace the path of humility. We serve an eternal God, and we know He has our backs no matter what kind of mountains we face. Most times we get to the place of humility through trials of fire and heartache. Psalm 34:18

says, *"The Lord is near to those who have a broken heart..."* (NKJV). He will be by our side; we just have to make sure we take Him at His Word! He will perform it.

Love has humility in it (see 1 Pet. 5:5). Love is not proud, love doesn't hold a record of wrongs, love is not jealous (see 1 Cor. 13:1-13). I have been guilty of these wrong actions and emotions before. Like everyone, I deal with issues, but I have learned to depend on God for everything that comes my way. It doesn't matter if it's negative or positive, bad news or good news. The Bible says we must guard our hearts and spirits (see Prov. 4:23), which I emphasized in Chapter One. We must guard our spirits or the enemy will have a field day with our minds and thoughts. Not every thought that comes into our mind is ours. The main ploy of the devil is to cast fiery darts (thoughts) into our minds in order to break down our faith (see Eph. 6:16).

Counterfeit Christians, who come to us in sheep's clothing, assuredly have polyester for wool, fangs for teeth, and paws for feet. In this age we are living in, we have to be aware and watchful of the counterfeits; sometimes they are not alone. They may even be among a leader in a church who is not well informed of their secret insolence, impudence, and trickery. We must be aware of these types of spirits in people while walking with discernment and a lowly attitude. We will always go further in the invisible when we do, manifesting into the natural for all to see Christ's Spirit radiating from us.

OBEDIENCE IS THE KEY

Our thoughts in life, as "fallen people," have caused wars, fights, strife, gossip, discord, pain, and everything else that is evil and negative in the world. We must read, pray, worship, and praise God every chance we get. Doing these things is how I have overcome with the help of the Holy Spirit, whom I have learned to love so much.

Show Him that you love Him with every thing you have in your heart. Thank Him always because He is so good. He will help you to worship when you don't know how or are having trouble doing so. Just keep reaching the heart of your Father, and He will help you learn to deal with the issues that come your way. This is an everyday process. It is not over until you are gone to Heaven or the rapture takes place. Jesus is your friend when you need Him to be, and I'm confident you desire that kind of friendship. This is a sign of loving Him: adore His commandments and obey (see 1 John 5:3); read His Word, meditating on it night and day, regardless of whether you feel like it or not. Learn to call to Him, "Hosanna!" when things are falling apart and you do not have any money in your bank account to pay for anything. Run to Him in your troubles, and run to Him when things are good. If you remain in Him, you will do well and accomplish many things.

In the past, relatives and believers in the Body of Christ have challenged me negatively and given me wrong information, but I learned to forgive and love every one of them, regardless of what they have done. Forgiveness is such a *huge* factor in the Church. Trials and tests that come through other people can become wearying and hectic to new believers, who must rely on the Lord for guidance and courage. He is always with us. He said, *"I will never leave you nor forsake you"* (Heb. 13:5). If we do right by God and follow His commandments, we prove we love Him (see 1 Sam. 15:22; 1 John 5:3). His commands are not grievous or painful (see 1 John 5:3); He knows when we love Him with all our hearts, minds, strength, bodies, souls, and spirits that we will do what He says. Obedience is the key.

CAST YOUR CARES

Even though some may see God's love as weakness, they have to realize that He will only endure so much before His judgment falls on them. This is why He has given us the manuscript to walk in His statutes and will. His mercy endures forever (see 1 Chron. 16:34); this is one reason why my soul cries out to God. His goodness is so wonderful and impeccable, not just because He is a giver of all things. I have learned to love Him and recognize His goodness regardless of whether I am living in plenty or in want. We must take that into consideration without complaining and murmuring (see Phil. 2:14). We must learn to cast our cares upon the Lord because He really does care about us (see 1 Pet. 5:7). *"Cast your burden on the Lord, and He shall sustain you; He shall never permit the righteous to be moved"* (Ps. 55:22 NKJV).

When we cast our cares on Him, no matter what the issue is, we must not take it back by worrying. This is how we take it back—by constantly speaking about it and holding on to it even after we have released it. God is greater than we can ever imagine. Worry is the absence of hope and faith. Always asking questions about how God is going to take care of our problems is also a type of "taking it back." If we continue to worry in this manner, it's a sign of doubt. (See James 1:5-8.) He will never leave us, though on occasion it may feel like He's not around.

*Let your conduct be without covetousness; be content with such things as you have. For He Himself has said, **I will never leave you nor forsake you** (Hebrews 13:5 NKJV).*

INTEGRITY: WHAT IS IT?

For years in church, I had Sunday friends who promised that they would be there for me no matter what. We traded phone numbers and email addresses, but not much real intimacy came from it. I say Sunday friends because they were just that. Always on Sunday after service they wanted to know how my family and I were doing. I would think to myself, *If you would call me like I call you, you would know how we are.*

There are many examples of rejection-fueled behavior and lack of integrity in the Body of Christ. This may seem or feel insignificant, but many people have left churches because no one would talk to them or say hello. It does affect the heart of the Image-Bearer (Christian). When individuals act with a lack of integrity on a constant basis, it tells me a lot about them. If I am always reaching out, but no one reaches back, that behavior is called a lack of integrity. Certainly it is not always a sign of, "I really don't care," or an "out of sight, out of mind" philosophy. I can see past the artificial attitude and the church face of a synthetic spirit.

The Lord doesn't agree with this kind of behavior. We all serve the same God, so we must treat each other like we matter. We must be men and women of our word. If we say we are going to do something, we must do just that. If we are not able to act upon our word, then we should let the person know. For example, if I was working for an employer, I wouldn't say I was going into work and then not show up. I would make sure that I called my boss; otherwise, I would not be employed very long.

Jesus wants us to be a community of people who hold on to our words. We all have our days of not being able to carry out what we say, and that's OK at times, but integrity is very important in the Body of Christ. We cannot say something and not mean it. We must go forward with keeping our appointments and obligations without deviating as much as possible. And when we cannot fulfill our commitment or make the appointment, we must be courteous enough to call and inform people.

Here's another example. Say a man has a son from a previous relationship; the child is anxious, excited, and ready to spend time with his father, but the father ends up not showing up. Not only will the boy be deeply hurt (especially if this is a repeated occurrence), but it will not be long before he stops believing his father. This can generate contention between the child and father as well as between the separated mother and father. This kind of thinking and irresponsibility can bring problems into a person's life as a whole, if not dealt with quickly.

Here's what the Bible says about the importance of integrity:

> *The righteous man walks in his integrity; his children are blessed after him* (Proverbs 20:7 NKJV).

> *Better is the poor who walks in his integrity...* (Proverbs 19:1 NKJV).

The integrity of the upright will guide them... (Proverbs 11:3 NKJV).

So he shepherded them according to the integrity of his heart, and guided them by the skillfulness of his hands (Psalm 78:72 NKJV).

Judge me, O Lord; for I have walked in mine integrity: I have trusted also in the Lord; therefore I shall not slide (Psalm 26:1).

I HAVE YOU ON MY MIND

According to our standards, we think we know better than God when it comes to knowing what would be best for us. When God calls us to His ministry, the pursuit begins. He's trying to get something to us, not take from us. There are many Scripture passages that prove His wisdom (see Prov. 2:1-9). His mind is beyond human comprehension. However, He has given us His Spirit to help us understand just enough of His intelligence so that we can partake of it and come into a more profound understanding. According to Dr. Caroline Leaf, this is the God who created our minds to be able to contain 3 million years of storage! Imagine His mind!

Before your brokenness period visits you, pray always, especially for God to give you the strength, grace, and power of the Holy Ghost to go through it and endure. In Psalm 23:4, it does *not* say, *"Though I **stay** in the valley..."* but rather, *"Though I walk **through** the valley...."* You can make it! Jesus constantly looks after you and advocates to the Father on your behalf when you go through the valley of adversity (see Rom. 8:27, 34). You are *never* alone! It is awesome to hear, "I am going through something right now." Operative word, *through*. Praise the Lord you are going through, rather then staying and wallowing in it. Keep this in the center of your thoughts, "This too shall pass."

IS IT WORTH IT?

Is it worth it? Yes!

You will be like gold when He is done with you. "Ready and willing" will become your motto. People will start to notice a change in your life and character. In the end, it will be wonderful to see and experience. When you look back at your life, you will say, "I cannot believe I went through that. I endured, and I am still here." You will be better than before, much closer to the likeness of Christ.

It won't be you, but God Himself who assists you to be a man or woman of humility. And in this humility, you will be able to stand and receive correction, and others will sense that you are approachable and easier to talk to. Once you have allowed brokenness to come, He can pour out the sweet-smelling oil of anointing on your spirit. Your heart of stone conforms into the heart of flesh that Christ would desire. The Holy Spirit can do His will easier, without any additional obstacles against Him. You will be able to listen to God and hear others more clearly. The Lord is able to speak to you and guide you. Communication with people will become easier as your meekness gives God glory. Meekness is power under control.

DAD, WHERE ARE YOU?

Speaking about meekness and being lowly was a very long process for me. I have cried and yelled with ceaseless tears to get where I am today. The pain and suffering I had to bear were agonizing and extremely lonely. I experienced betrayals, loneliness, let downs, beatings, bullying, my own foolishness, misery, lack of love, problems I created for myself, accusations, being molested and raped at the age of 6, and being homeless with my mother and two younger brothers for almost a year in the streets of a city where I knew no one. It caused me to build a huge wall in my heart to prevent anyone from penetrating it and seeing the person I really was.

Periodically, my father would show up in my life. I can remember maybe three times I have seen my father. At the ages of 7, 12, and 21 for four to seven days at the most each time. My father was unaware of the negative situations that I had to go through, especially when I became homeless. Being homeless caused everything to be stripped from me until I had nothing but a thin black trench coat on my back to protect me from negative ten-degree weather in the middle of winter. I was walking and wondering every day where God was in all of this, and where my natural father was.

In my heart of hearts, I had to start all over again from scratch since I was stripped until nothing remained. In many ways, this broke me, and yet I was hard-hearted like Pharaoh (see Exod. 7:13). I thought to myself, *Not only did my natural father abandon me, but my spiritual Father abandoned me also.* Reality for me was not real at all; changing the course of my ways took time. A few months down the road of my misfortunes, this thought entered my mind, *I am not the only one going through trials of fire, testing, and hardship. There must be others weathering something similar to me.* I had to reason with myself, convincing myself with the fact that there were people in the world who would have loved to trade places with me because what I was experiencing looked and sounded like nothing compared to their difficulties. When I read the Book of Job, it made a lot of sense to me; I understood why he would ask God, *Why?* There was so much that Job had to go through.

This was not just a "few months thing" or a "year thing"; this was my whole entire life! All of my life has been one huge trial without me seeing or experiencing an oasis. People in the world, my friends, and my family didn't understand me. All along, there was a call on my life, and I didn't even know it. At the same time, I was feeling the four walls of loneliness close in on me. I wondered, *Where is my Dad in Heaven?* Eventually, the Lord did show up. He had been visiting me ever since I was a young child in the South Bronx, New York, sleeping in my little bed. When I received that word later in my life, that Jesus was visiting me when I was a young child, it made a great amount of sense. My Daddy, after all, has been there through all the hell I had to experience. The spiritual ingredient to all of this was to forgive my parents, God, and most importantly, myself.

PROTECTING THE ANOINTING

Have you ever had anyone come into your circle of friends who never went through hell, like you have, but who tried to preach to you or tell you what to do? If you have, welcome to a club I like to call, "I Have Gone Through Enough."

I tell you the truth; I went through so much in my life it was ridiculous! I am so thankful for the mercy and grace God has shown us. *"Those who love much are the ones who have been forgiven much"* (Luke 7:47). As you spend much time with sisters and brothers in the Lord, you can see Luke chapter 7:47 come alive. In the sense Christians haven't come close to what you have gone through in your life trying to disprove your own experiences. When you love the Lord much it's because He has forgiven you for so many things you have done wrong in your life. In return, you desire to love the Lord with everything you've got! However, certain Believers haven't even touched the surface of your past sufferings to understand you enough but yet they desire to teach you how to overcome your situation. Plus, they may not love their God as much as you do. My question is: So what can such people teach us? How are they able to minister to us when all they have gone through is not being able to put gas in their cars or having a hard time trying to park closer to the stores entrance? What has God really delivered them from? People who have experienced real hell in their lives will give Jesus all the glory and honor for fixing their mess, thanking Him daily for saving them. Not to try to state (whether a friend or associate) will bend over backward for the Lord, or you, when you can see clearly past their agenda.

This goes to show we must be very meticulous about who we allow to take part in our lives. Some may seem they are after our best interests at first, when in turn they are insensitive, conniving, having other plans to hurt you. It may not be physical; a person can hurt you spiritually as well. We must walk vigilantly and caution ourselves against spiritual leeches; they will suck us dry until every ounce of energy is absorbed. Some believers would cling to us because they realize who we are in the Spirit and the gift that has been bestowed upon our lives. They make it their goal to leech from the anointing, wanting the easy way.

This reminds me of a time when a particular man wanted to have the anointing God has put on my life, knowing full well the entire misfortune I had to suffer. I said, "So, you want this anointing?"

The man said, "Yeah, I want it now!"

I said, "OK, Lord, I pray that he gets molested and raped, death to visit his close friends and family members, betrayal to come his way, drown in loneliness, be misrepresented, misunderstood, a year of homelessness, days of hunger, days of thirst, no showers, getting beat up, to be almost killed in a house fire, divorced, abandoned by his father, to be almost murdered after witnessing a shooting and seeing their faces, living in fear they might return. I pray that he will be put in jail, be gossiped about, falsely accused and jailed, his mother to get beaten in front of him. Lord, I pray that his parents would become alcoholics and drug users."

He pulled away from me and said, "Whoa! Wait a minute! Apostle Luis, don't pray for some craziness like that in my life!"

I said, "Sir, didn't you say you wanted my anointing?"

He said arrogantly, "Yes I did."

"Well sir, if you are not willing to go through these things and more the way I did, then you are not willing to pay the price that I had to pay. The anointing of God costs! It is not free!"

We must be cautious of those who want what we have and who try to drain us every chance they get. They want to steal, kill, and destroy what God has implanted deep down inside of us—pulling on us, fishing, trying to get to know our character and motives. We must stay away from the artificial and counterfeit Christians who are trying to consume us in the spirit! Please forgive me for my boldness, but this is one of the reasons why I wrote about this topic. It's dangerous in these evil times. I know some will not go through all this just to have the anointing, but I was trying to prove a point. Again, to make my point clear, we mustn't allow just anyone to come into our lives with harmful agendas with what God has instilled in us just because they said God told them to be part of our lives. We must be careful in these perilous times.

> But know this, that in the last days perilous times will come: **For men will be lovers of themselves**, lovers of money, boasters, proud, blasphemers, disobedient to parents, unthankful, unholy, unloving, unforgiving, slanderers, without self-control, brutal, despisers of good, traitors, headstrong, **haughty**, lovers of pleasure rather than lovers of God, **having a form of godliness but denying its power**. And from such people turn away (2 Timothy 3:1-5 NKJV).

THE PRIDE OF LIFE

Pride in some ways can be OK, according to the way our clothes fit or the way we look or as a sense of self-worth and self-esteem. Of course, we can be proud of the way we look as long as it doesn't turn into something that is totally rejected by God; then it has become something else. The

Holy Scriptures state that God hates pride (see Prov. 6:16 BBE). The word *pride* has the word *ride* in it. Pride will take us for a ride to a place we do not want to go. It will not be long before we complain about wanting to get off, but most times, it is too late. When people walk in the spirit of pride, we can discern the spirit simply by being around them because the Holy Spirit tells us. If we're not sure, we can just pay close attention to what kind of tree they are and the fruit they produce. Some fruit has worms in the center, so we must be very careful.

> *Pride goes before destruction, and a haughty spirit before a fall. Better to be of a humble spirit with the lowly, than to divide the spoil with the proud* (Proverbs 16:18-19 NKJV).

> *By pride comes nothing but strife, but with the well advised is wisdom* (Proverbs 13:10 NKJV).

Jesus was tempted by the devil with a question associated with the "pride of life." As I have studied the Word of the Lord, I came to know Him on a deeper, more intimate level. I see what pride and its spiritual cousins (arrogance, conceit, pleasure, self-gratification, and smugness) were doing to me and in all of my relationships. Before I began to perceive my "Valley of Brokenness," I had to step into my own life first to see what others saw in me, with the help of the Spirit of God. He helped me to see all the junk that was killing me on the inside, which I did not discern before. If we do not draw near to God so God can draw near to us, it will suffocate our relationships with others, too.

Having vision is not the same as having sight, and this is part of being Kingdom-minded, which I will write about later. As we learn how to be vigilant and sober in the things of the spirit that come our way, especially related to the vision of our leaders, God will take us to different heights in the Spirit that will bring us to our knees. We will have no other choice but to fight satan and his minions with the Word of God. When believers in Christ come against this celebrated idea, that the enemy thinks he has us cornered, this is when strong opposition by prayer will start on the part of the Believer. This is what Jesus perceived from the words satan spoke to Him (see Luke 4:5-8). Jesus was probably thinking to Himself, *satan, you are such a fool. How are you going to give me something that is already mine?* Imagine how I would look stealing a brand new television out of someone's home and then trying to sell it back to them? It's absolutely foolish. The devil offered to Jesus the kingdoms, cities, people, houses, and such—which *already belonged to Jesus*—knowing in his mind that Jesus already owned them. Jesus would not bow down to satan; He recognized his pride and self-centered desires of impiety and malevolence.

> *Again, the devil took Him up on an exceedingly high mountain, and showed Him all the kingdoms of the world and their glory. And he said to Him, "All these things I will give You if You will fall down and worship me." Then Jesus said to him, "Away with you, Satan! For it is written, 'You shall worship the Lord your God, and Him only you shall serve.'" Then the devil left Him, and behold, angels came and ministered to Him* (Matthew 4:8-11 NKJV).

Pride is all about *me* and what *I* can get out of the deal. Pride destroys without the concern of others. Self-gratification in all areas of life is satan's evil fill. Caution should be our middle name because pride is a spirit of leviathan. Beware of that spirit; it will eradicate anyone, saved or unsaved. In the end, we know God Almighty will punish that spirit. The Bible says, *"In that day the Lord with his sore and great and strong sword shall punish **leviathan** the piercing serpent, even leviathan that crooked serpent..."* (Isa. 27:1) and *"You broke the heads of **Leviathan** in pieces, and gave him as food to the people inhabiting the wilderness"* (Ps. 74:14 NKJV).

Self-importance and smugness always take from others and are constantly greedy for more. Those with these attitudes are never satisfied with the now. Impatience is the cousin of pride. If we are not aware and on guard, these spirits will creep in and tear down what we hold dear. For example, a man is driving, but a driver in front of him is slowing him down. He keeps beeping the horn, trying to get around, feeling anger rising up inside; finally, as he passes the vehicle, he gives the other person half of a peace sign. That is pride combined with a spirit of anger. The Bible tells us to become angry, but not to sin (see Eph. 4:26).

Here's another scenario. A woman is sitting at a traffic light, and she's getting frustrated because it's not changing fast enough. That is a sign of pride. It's the attitude, "I want it now; I don't care about anyone else's wants but my own!" I am not talking about emergencies or things of that nature. I'm talking about when you didn't *have to* rush, but you rush anyway. What happened to letting patience have its perfect work in you? The Bible says, *"But let patience have its perfect work, that you may be perfect and complete, lacking nothing"* (James 1:4 NKJV). These are the little signs of pride in our lives, *"just like the little foxes"* (Song of Sol. 2:15). Sometimes we try to look for the big things to see what a person deals with, when in reality, we must never lose focus to the little foxes which are the little problems that may arise discreetly causing you to lose focus on God's promises for your life. We have to be prudent and wise in the Spirit, letting God help us to be more like Him and to break the spirit of pride off of our lives.

My wife and I knew a couple who would never pray for patience because they were afraid it would only bring lots of trouble and tribulation. That was the spirit of fear speaking to them. Jesus will never give us patience, but will allow various oppositions to work in our favor by bringing us through storms. When those battles and conflicts come our way, it will not feel like it's training us while it is happening, but it will be working in our favor, and when it is finished, we will then thank God for it. In the end, we will have the spirit of patience, enabling us to deal with an irritated or angry spouse, a terrible boss, or any difficulty that may come our way. We will be trained in being slow to anger and being peaceful, loving, and much more simply through being patient.

Now that I am wiser, by the grace of Almighty God, I see that I had the wrong attitude toward the idea of not praying for "patience" because it not only violated James 1:4, but it also could have prevented me from totally breaking of the spirit of haughtiness and from attaining a oneness of peace and meekness. Now that I have learned to be patient, I know now being patient was a very important part of my brokenness that was necessary for change.

ME, MYSELF, AND I

Warning! Pride is a Spirit Killer! In the past, humility was not my strong point. I was very controlling in my marriage, with my children, and toward others. There were times when pride came and raised its ugly head, and I had to fight against myself with the power of the Spirit. Now, it's not as bad as it used to be. The more time we spend with God and in His Word, the better our attitudes get. I must *always* rely on the Holy Spirit everyday to help me because I do fall short when pride arises. Always seeking a way out and running to the altar in prayer and fasting helps me in my need. Keeping this ugly spirit as far away from me as possible helps me to see clearly. Pride doesn't like anyone telling it what to do. People who are walking in pride feel like they do not need any help because they have everything under control and figured out.

We must be aware that pride can bring other spirits into our lives if we don't deal with it immediately. We need to realize that we deal with things that are in "high places" (see Eph. 6:12). I almost destroyed my second marriage because of not being willing to just submit to my wife and respect her. I drove my first wife to a different person because I was cold in my heart and in my thoughts—wanting things to go a certain direction, which was a major focus for me. My mother also didn't want me in her house. The way I spoke to her and dishonored her was very sharp and piercing. Pride was the bed I slept on, and rebellion was my pillow, while stubbornness was my blanket. My life has been a very rough and hard path; I stepped on a lot of toes and burned bridges with my actions and words. I would love to meet the person who said, "Sticks and stones may break my bones, but words can never hurt me." The truth is, words hurt, destroying the lives of people by the thousands. If only graves could speak.

As we read Scripture, encounter the parable about the prodigal son (see Luke 15:11-32). I was the son who stood at home and also the other living a riotous life. Friends did not want to be around me. There were times when our friends loved to hang around my wife as long as I wasn't around. That really bothered and hurt me—knowing I was a born-again Christian just like them. With all of my being, I tried to figure out why others eluded me, but it really boggled my mind. Seeing the truth about my behavior was hard for me to grasp, and part of me just didn't want to see what they saw, yearning to stay in my denial.

I would read my Bible and then condemn my wife for not reading, praying with all these sophisticated words just to judge my wife for not speaking the same way. A heart of a Pharisee and the mind of a Sadducee in me took a toll on her spirit. My wife, Michelle, kept it to herself for many years. She didn't want to hurt me by telling me what our friends had said about me. She knew that she would have been my primary target. I would have blamed her for allowing others to talk about me, wondering why they didn't confront me about the issue instead of telling her.

Now I see; looking back, I believe the spirit of anger I had would not have taken correction that easily. Several others were afraid of me also because I know Wing Chun Kung Fu and was a Grandmaster of my own martial arts system that I had studied and trained in for 30 years. It was not my goal to make my family and my brothers and sisters in the Lord afraid of me. But in my pride, I just couldn't realize what was going on in my soul. Writing this hurts me even now, knowing I was so hard on my wife, my kids, my mother, my brothers, and my friends. This was my life circle of trust with my relatives, but all I was doing was hurting them.

I questioned God. With tears and a broken spirit, I yelled from the top of my lungs, "Lord, who am I? Tell me who I am? Tell me what I can do? Is this who I have become? Does my life stop here? What is my true identity? Will I ever know my true purpose in this life? Why do I keep hurting everyone who gets near me? If this is who I am, I no longer want it!"

Suicidal thoughts began to flood my mind, trying to convince me that I would never change and that, by taking my life, I would stop my own hurt and would no longer be able to hurt others. The trash of my past came to haunt me as these old feelings started to rise in my mind. I thought about jumping off a bridge that was near my home and contemplated walking in front of a truck. Besieged with evil imaginations, I thought to myself, *Maybe that would help the situation. My wife could marry someone who is good to her. My mother would be happier if I were just gone. Who needs me anyway, I'm a failure!*

Promises would flow from my lips, but people would just look at me with doubt. The nights I had of tears and heartache will never leave my mind. I was overwhelmed by fear that one day my wife would come home and say it's over. I dreaded my friends emailing me, declaring an end to their visits to our home. I feared my mom calling and saying, "You are no longer welcome in my house." I had to run to the Lord for new breath, for new life! Everything around me was falling apart. Crying out to God to change me hurt as well, and His process of changing me ached all the more. I found myself wondering if there would be a light at the end of the burrow of my inner man. I wanted to trade it all in for a new character and a clean heart.

Although I was saved, my mentality was not renewed. I had hidden anger, bitterness, and resentment, and I wanted to be compensated by everyone. I especially wanted my mother to pay me back what she had stolen years before. I wanted her to pay for the days she abandoned me and caused me to be homeless, and I wanted her to pay for allowing me to be molested, even though I kept silent about it for 27 years and didn't tell her. I was not thinking logically, but from a place of wounding.

It's critically important for us to realize that change is possible and that the Lord needs us to be broken. During that time in my life, I was not paying attention to what the apostle Peter said about our character toward others:

> *Finally, all of you be of one mind, having compassion for one another; love as brothers, be tenderhearted, be courteous; not returning evil for evil or reviling for reviling, but on the contrary blessing, knowing that you were called to this, that you may inherit a blessing. For "He who would love life and see good days, let him refrain his tongue from evil, and his lips from speaking deceit. Let him turn away from evil and do good; Let him seek peace and pursue it. For the eyes of the Lord are on the righteous, and His ears are open to their prayers; but the face of the Lord is against those who do evil"* (1 Peter 3:8-12 NKJV).

RENEWED AND ACCEPTED

When I read those words out loud, it pierced my spirit. I thought, *There is so much that happened in my life, but I am sure others have gone through much worse.* I began to think of stories I had heard that were unbearable to even consider. I thought, *If they could survive that horrific life, then I can endure mine and make a change for the better.* My life of obedience was on a separate mantle in the spirit, meaning that God holds my obedience at a higher standard since Jesus called me to be His end-time Apostle. And since apostles are first in the Church, it has not always been easy. Walking back into reality with anticipation and optimism was very difficult. I wasn't sure if anyone would give me a second chance. Challenges that were manifesting in ways I couldn't even articulate with words engulfed me. The Lord took me and honored my questions by putting me into a blaze of transformation. It is a very hot place to be in. Afterward, with much prayer, fasting, and obedience to the Lord and His Word, I was able to listen for the first time. The spirit of anger would not overtake me like it used to.

A renewed mind and heart took charge of my motives. My wife and I had a long talk. It was the best talk I ever had with her and the kids. An absolution was needed in that area, and it had blessed me. I did not know how much damage I had caused with that murdering, prideful spirit and attitude. I went back to my mother and apologized to her with all of my soul and asked for forgiveness. I took full responsibility for my actions and asked my brothers and sisters in Christ for their exoneration. Amnesty was very much needed from all whom I held dear.

There is so much more I could write about this, but my point is that God can change a heart that's willing. No matter the concern or need, the Holy Spirit will run to your rescue. Being able to praise God with my whole heart feels so good; I am no longer in bondage to those things. Everyday I wake up by the grace of God and start my day refreshed and renewed, never looking back or returning to that man I once was. Admitting that I sinned against my own family and friends has helped me appreciate and realize new mercies in Christ. I would not even blame them if they did not forgive me, but I praise God that they did. I had to know myself all over again, and the Holy Ghost came and filled me (and He still is filling me to this day). Thank you, Jesus!

DEAD MAN WALKING

After the change in me, old friends from the past would still come up to me and try to incite the old me. With refinement and gentleness, I would turn them down and say, "Sir, please don't try to resurrect a man who died a long time ago; that Luis Lopez no longer exists." The cool thing is, I didn't have to give them Bible passages, plead the blood, or give them an entire church program explaining how I had changed for the better. Just something simple would suffice. When the Lord does a perfect work in us, we will have the enemy bring people up from our past to rekindle the *old person*. We must not hesitate to say that the *old person* no longer exists. We will thank ourselves later for the trouble we have avoided, and we will bring glory to God! We should never take away His glory for the change in our lives; He deserves every single word of praise for it. Amen.

PRAYER

My Precious Father, how I long to change for the better. Purify my heart and embrace me my Lord. I will always be yours. Knowing this truth of always being yours can change many things in my life because you are with me. According to your Word, I am more than a conqueror as long as I follow your Word and be obedient to you. Thank you Lord for protecting me from those who tried to harm me and my family. And right now I also pray that you continue to bring peace into my home and into the hearts and minds of my family. Bring peace also to me my Lord. There is no one in this world like you God. I have tried other things in my life before I knew you, and now that I know You, my life has never been the same and I am eternally grateful. I pray that you continue to watch over my family now and forever. You do comfort the comfortless. Although at times it may not seem like it, it is true nevertheless. Help me to follow hard after you and be broken so you may use me mightily. Sharpen my gifts so I can be a blessing to the Body of Christ. May I always be in your presence to hear your beautiful voice clearer and clearer, in Your precious Son's name, Jesus. Thank you my Lord for hearing my prayer. Amen.

CHAPTER THREE

The Beginning of Wisdom

The fear of the Lord is the beginning of wisdom....
—PSALM III:IO

The fear of the Lord, which is the beginning of God's holy wisdom, is no longer demonstrated in our day and age. We are taking His commandments out of governmental and federal areas. We are telling our children in schools to stop praying. We are teaching the next generation that the Bible is just a book of fairy tales and stories. One thing we have to understand, no one can ever take prayer out of schools, because when we think a prayer (and even before we begin to speak), He hears us.

Ironically, many Christians have been taught that the devil can hear them thinking. Therefore, believers feel they shouldn't pray in their heads, because they have been programmed to assume satan knows what they are saying to

God. I have never found that in the pages of the Bible. Instead, our God is the only one who can hear and see our hearts and minds thinking:

> *Then hear Thou in heaven Thy dwelling place, and forgive, and do, and give to every man according to his ways, **whose heart Thou knowest; (for Thou, even Thou only, knowest the hearts of all the children of men)*** (1 Kings 8:39).

> *And the Spirit of the Lord fell upon me, and said unto me, Speak; Thus saith the Lord; Thus have ye said, O house of Israel: **for I know the things that come into your mind, every one of them*** (Ezekiel 11:5).

> *For there is not a word in my tongue, but, lo, O Lord, Thou knowest it altogether* (Psalm 139:4).

From Genesis 9:2 to Revelation 19:5, you will find the word *fear* appearing in the Bible 501 times, with different meanings, interpretations, and connotations. The most important is the fear of the Lord. We are not told to have fear of anything or anyone else or to fear praying. But the fear of the Lord is different. The fear of God is more of a reverential fear since you love Him, as opposed to fear that torments and paralyzes individuals. The beginning of wisdom will help us stay in position where we need to be and also will help us put things in their proper angle. In order to categorize ourselves to be in a place of respect and honor toward the Lord, we have to embrace His Word daily. Here are three passages to heighten His point of view:

*My son, if you receive my words, and treasure my commands within you, so that you incline your ear to wisdom, and apply your heart to understanding; yes, if you cry out for discernment, and lift up your voice for understanding, if you seek her as silver, and search for her as for hidden treasures; then you will understand **the fear of the Lord**, and find the knowledge of God* (Proverbs 2:1-5 NKJV).

If My people who are called by My name will humble themselves, and pray and seek My face, and turn from their wicked ways, then I will hear from heaven, and will forgive their sin and heal their land (2 chronicles 7:14 NKJV).

...If you walk in My statutes, execute My judgments, keep all My commandments, and walk in them, then I will perform My word with you... (1 Kings 6:12 NKJV).

If people don't fear God, whether they are Christians or unbelievers, they will never come to an apex of total life, and that total life is only by following the narrow steps of repentance and obedience that Jesus outlined for all of us.

Why would anyone listen to a God who commands all people everywhere to follow His statutes, His footsteps, if there is no fear? In people's minds, there are no limits, no fear of God, and no warning signs of consequence. *Fear* and the *Lord*, to them, are only bywords of false hope, and they believe they have no perpetuity after they pass away. Most have been taught that we are like animals, just here to live, work, die, and then go into a "no consciousness" sleep and be transported into an epoch without end. These evil philosophies have no solid foundation in real truth and the hard facts of real conformity. Fearing God helps us keep track so we don't have to keep falling into the snares of satan's schemes. The Holy Spirit will always be there for us to assist and sanction us into newness of living, at the same time defending us when the flood waters of dissension try to step over our boundaries.

REPENT AND BE RESTORED

Unfortunately, many leaders today are not listening with the heart of fear toward God in these last days. The Spirit of God is not taken seriously, but as a joke. Too many people are saying they are on the side of the Lord, but all they are transmitting is a distorted outlook into the church, with the signs of a Jezebel spirit and a Judas Iscariot spirit. We must be aware of the enemy and know what our true purpose is in life. If we are not, our "greatness" within our spirits will die and may never manifest or come to fruition! Time is drawing near, and the judgment to all people is closer than it has ever been. We must take this walk very seriously and get right in the sight of the Lord.

In the words of John the Baptist, "Repent! His Kingdom draws near!" (See Matt. 3:1.) This is not a game to be toying with; this is our lives, and it is especially urgent for those of us who are leaders or ministers of the Gospel. If leaders fall away, or trample on the Word, there is a punishment that is much greater than that of those who hold a lower position in the spirit referring to how much they know of God, according to the Bible (see Heb. 10:29; Luke 12:48). The grace of God is being trampled underfoot, and His mercy is being taken advantage of. His Spirit will strive with humanity for only so long. We all must be reminded that it is a terrible thing to fall into the hands of the living God (see Heb. 10:31). Let's not take the Lord for granted. We must repent! We are about to meet the King, whether in death or in the catching away, and we must repent, no matter the circumstances. We must repent so we can be restored back to Him in this everlasting love affair!

THE OTHER SIDE OF GOD

God is our Father, my Father. When are we going to show Him through our lives that we truly do love Him? We must fear God! Ultimately, we will give an account to Him (perhaps one day soon), and we do not want to be left behind when the rapture occurs, or worse, enter into the resurrection of the wicked dead, as the wicked will be judged at the white throne judgment (see 1 Thess. 4:16-18; Rev. 20:11-15). Our souls and spirits are going to stand in front of Christ (see Rom. 14:10). Every soul and spirit from every person will *never* die because we are eternal beings. Those who do not accept Christ will not physically die as we know death, But will suffer in hell, which is considered a second death of the spirit (see Matt. 10:28; Rev. 21:8). Those of us who do accept Christ will live forever with Him in Heaven. It's up to us to choose while we are alive in this world where we want to spend eternity.

The reason God sends those who evade His Son to hell is because there is nowhere else to send them, but into an eternal torment and total separation from the Master of creation (see Rev. 20:15). I plead with so many in the ministry to get it right and stop dabbling with sin, and they consider me to be too spiritual or too righteous. I respond that we can never be spiritual enough. The Word says to walk after the Spirit and not the flesh (see Rom. 8:1).

Can you say that you are ready to stand before Him if He came for you now? Or will you barely make it? You have to have a diligent spirit to do the work God has set before you. Your works will turn into hay and stubble if genuine love is not portrayed in your spirit and soul: *"If his work is burned up, he will suffer the loss. However, **he will be saved, though it will be like going through a fire"** (1 Cor. 3:15 GW).

We must walk after the Spirit! Yes, we fall short and mess up sometimes, but at the same time, we must recognize how we are behaving so that we do not stay where satan and the flesh want us. We need to make sure that God is pleased with us. I desire to hear, *"Well done, good and faithful servant"* (Matt. 25:21, 23).

"God is love" (1 John 4:8), and the love that He gives echoes throughout the pages of the Bible; we must understand that this is where His heart is. God is head over heels in love with us. We must dare to be relentless with spreading the gospel of God to anyone we see without being weary, since time is getting short. Our reward is coming for all the concerns we had to face while on this earth. Barely making it and not putting our entire hearts and minds to serving Him will not work. That is not going to do it; we need to get it together. We all have it in us to do it; we just need to choose.

Don't wait until Judgment Day to decide to make a change for the better. If you do, it will be too late! His judgments are swift and very sudden. If the *waiting* comes to full fruition and you are caught in the act of rebellion and are not repentant, He will have you depart from His presence: *"And then will I profess unto them, I never knew you: depart from Me, ye that work iniquity"* (Matt. 7:23). I implore you to put a lifestyle of holiness and reverence into action now; thus, His hand will not have to weigh you down and press you into the center of the earth. You can't live like God in public, and act like the devil at home. You must be striving for godliness all the time, especially when you are alone. This shows the Lord and yourself what your true character is and where you are in your spirit.

Too much has been arising in the churches behind closed doors. Jesus is looking for a house, a temple, without spot or blemish (see Eph. 5:27). Those who do not fit this description will be left behind. We must not take this lightly. There are enough counterfeits calling themselves Christians as it is; we must not add our names to this list of artificiality. As Jesus said to one of the churches in Revelation, we must be on fire for God or cold for God, but not mingle in between; it will anger the Lord in a very somber manner. *"So then, because you are lukewarm, and neither cold nor hot, I will vomit you out of My mouth"* (Rev. 3:16 NKJV).

Having spiritual role models will elevate you drastically, helping you to become more righteous. Remember, we should not be overly righteous or overly wicked. Solomon wrote very clearly about this destructive path.

> *Do not be overly righteous, nor be overly wise: Why should you destroy yourself? Do not be overly wicked, nor be foolish: Why should you die before your time?* (Ecclesiastes 7:16-17 NKJV)

WHICH ONE WILL WE CHOOSE?

A garment of salvation is different than a robe of righteousness (see Isa. 61:10). The difference between the "garment of salvation" and a "robe of righteousness" in my understanding is that the garment of salvation means you barely made it into Heaven therefore it will take you longer to get to God in His heavenly City; in contrast, the robe of righteousness allows you to approach the City of God a lot quicker because you actually were very obedient while you were living on earth. This was my understanding according to my experience of the heavenly visitation, which I will mention later in this book. Which one will we choose, the garment or the robe? We must put on the Lord Jesus Christ no matter what circumstances come our way. God desires to be first in our lives—before children, spouses, our jobs, and material things. Jesus has to be number one at all times. It is possible to put Him first. *"All things are possible for those who believe"* (Mark 9:23). We must get used to the fact that we have to *listen* to the prompting and voice of the Holy Spirit. God wants us to have reverential fear directed to Him, not as the world knows fear, but the way the Bible explains it. Where it states in Proverbs 9:10, *"The fear of the Lord is the beginning of wisdom and the knowledge of the holy is understanding."* A large number of people who profess they love God do not follow His sayings. Basically, not everyone who professes Christ is right with the Lord.

Notice what James says, *"Be a doer of the Word and not a hearer only deceiving yourself"* (James 1:22-25). We cannot just praise the Lord with our lips, honoring God in public while living a lie and being disobedient behind closed doors.

There is a lot of that going on already, and that is a perfect example of counterfeit Christianity. These people portray themselves in the limelight as holy and anointed, yet when no one is watching, they're living like satan. Loving God is an act of relational prayer. I understand that God is invisible, but we must spend time with Him just like we do with people—and we must do it with honesty and integrity in the sight of God and people. We are promised in Scripture that if we fear God, if we love Him and obey Him, we will live longer lives and become whole people (see Prov. 1:7; Prov. 3:1, 2; Prov. 10:27; John 14:15; Eph. 6:3).

Which will you choose—a garment of salvation or a robe of righteousness? What's the difference? In Proverbs, it says this about the importance of walking in righteousness:

> Hear, my son, and receive my sayings, and **the years of your life will be many**. I have taught you in the way of wisdom; I have led you in right paths. When you walk, your steps will not be hindered, and when you run, you will not stumble. Take firm hold of instruction, do not let go; keep her, for she is your life (Proverbs 4:10-13 NKJV).

The problem I see with kids, teenagers, and young adults today is that they don't even fear their parents, whom they can see, let alone God, whom they can't see. The Christ in us, the hope of glory (see Col. 1:27), can train them in the way they should go, and when they get older, they will not depart from it (see Prov. 22:6). This also applies to the unrighteous. If they train up children in wickedness, they will not depart from that, either. It's not true in all cases, but in many.

We must pay close attention to what God is saying to us! The whole duty of humanity is to fear God and follow hard after Him, obeying His Word. Jesus is that Word! *"Let us hear the conclusion of the whole matter: **Fear God**, and keep his commandments: for **this is the whole duty of man**"* (Eccles. 12:13).

KNOWN BY ASSOCIATION

We must associate with people who are powerful in the Lord. It's good for us to provoke wisdom and knowledge when the anointing is available. We must surround ourselves with those who bear good and lasting fruit. Fruit takes time to grow on a tree and expand, as well as develop seeds. In obedience, we will do the same—letting time pass so the seeds can grow in us as trees of maturity, and we will allow them to expand so that we will come into the character of that total man or woman of Christ we are called to be. This means we have been obedient and diligent to produce seed to plant into His Kingdom in order to reap a harvest of our righteousness in Christ.

This is not a sprint, but a relay. The race of faith is not given to the swift, but to the diligent. We hand the baton of God's Word brother-to-brother and sister-to-sister in order to encourage, edify, exhort, rebuke, and correct in love. This is especially true for apostles and prophets, who must, by the authority of the Most High, instruct, prophesy, and bring forth the Word to edify the Body. Believers need to honor the wisdom and understanding of these ministers who bring forth revelation to the Church Body, giving heed to and honoring these ministers.

As we do this, we will begin to become sensitive to what is needed in a particular season with the leading of the Spirit. I am astonished by how much we have veered from showing respect to ministers of God; too often reverence has not entered into the minds and spirits of believers. Reverential fear of the Lord is slowly dissipating, slowly vanishing, as well in the commitment to following the direction of the anointed leaders He ordains. We must position ourselves to bring into culmination what Christ has for us, and most of the time the Lord uses His ministers to do this.

We must not give up on ourselves or God's anointed leaders. Let's remember where God is coming from regarding His standards of holiness as He anoints the leaders in His Church and leads them into higher dimensions of ministry and power. The Bible says, *"He permitted no one to do them wrong; yes, He rebuked kings for their sakes, saying, 'Do not touch My anointed ones, and do My prophets no harm'"* (Ps. 105:14-15 NKJV). We must not violate this Scripture. Leaders who are being victimized by such pure foolishness should pray and then warn their people according to what the prophet David said.

PICK A SIDE AND COMPLY

Christians need to come under the hand of the Almighty and learn how to build a solid foundation of respectability and sanctity in order to have fullness and wholeness of life—with nothing missing or broken. Occasionally, circumstances might feel void of our Savior's presence; at times He may seem inaccessible to us, causing us to think that God is not real. But this is all deception from our flesh, the devil intensifying what we have already conjured up in our thoughts.

We must quote and read His Word daily; this is what puts us back into alignment with the Lord. Another key element is prayer, which helps us to get closer to God. Once we recognize that the reality of who God is comes through revelation and relationship, a stronger intimacy with Him will pervade our lives. We will be encompassed in the Lord's presence, with love and expectancy in holy fear, which will enable us to give the Lord true worship. God is a good God; He loves us and our families more than we could ever anticipate. In this realm we call the earth, prayer is our lifeline of liberty and power, reaching from this place to the place we call "mi casa"—our home, which is Heaven.

ABOVE YOUR STANDARDS

It has not entered into our hearts and minds how much the Savior really loves us (see 1 Cor. 2:9; Isa. 64:4). When we demonstrate to God that He is absolute number one in our lives (also showing others that He is number one), unequivocally, His blessings will begin to fall on us, and wherever we go, He will be there. His presence as the trinity—Father, Son, and Holy Spirit—will simply overtake us. He will dispatch angels to guard us all the days we have on earth, working for the Body of believers and those who are in desperate need of a Word of hope. The New Testament says, *"Men should always pray"* (Luke 18:1) and *"pray always without ceasing"* (1 Thess. 5:17). We must never give up hope, never stop having faith and believing in what has been spoken. We will reap quickly; payday will be here soon!

Let's meditate on these questions:

- How can we go on sinning, and not repent?

- How can we say we fear God and then do the opposite, knowing full well it is contrary to His will?

- Why do we so often break Yahweh's heart?

- We dishonor Him and hurt His feelings. We must stop! We can't live lifestyles of disobedience when the winds of rejection and trial start to overtake us. The real questions are:

- What are we going to do about our problems?

- Are we going to stand firm through pain and distress?

- What makes us think we are better than God that we are unwilling to suffer, though He suffered great pain for us?

Jesus, the Son of God, had to undergo the pain and agony of rejection, torment, and betrayal; many horrific events took place in His life. It pleased the Lord God to bring this judgment on His Son, understanding in His infinite wisdom what it would do for countless millions (probably billions) in the future (see Isa. 53:10). If we only could see what is coming on the day of Christ's return for the born-again saints who stay committed, centered, and focused; it's going to be captivating. For humankind to actually experience what's to come, a light must come on in the inside of us that enables us to listen to God.

Obey the Spirit of God to the best of your ability when He speaks to you. If you do not, a price will be paid as you continue to disprove what has been set before you. It will cost you all of eternity. Do not get curious to see what's on the other side of the valley of judgment; it is not appealing. His punishments are great because He is great. His love is great because He is great. His thoughts are not your thoughts, and His ways are not your ways, since He is great:

> *"For My thoughts are not your thoughts, nor are your ways My ways," says the Lord. "For as the heavens are higher than the earth, so are My ways higher than your ways, and My thoughts than your thoughts"* (Isaiah 55:8-9 NKJV).

Let's visualize for a moment a Christian man who is 6 feet tall. That is as high as he can think compared to the Lord's mental capacity. God thinks on a multi-dimensional mental level, far beyond humankind's aptitude. In High School, my teacher taught me that scientists and doctors who have studied the human brain say that we use 10 to 12 percent of our brain cells. And Albert Einstein, who was considered the smartest man in the world in his time, used 18 percent of his brain cells. His discovery of $E=mc^2$ led to the development of the atomic bomb. As distinguished as Einstein was, his brain capacity was no match for Noah's. It is believed that the antediluvian people of his day used both halves of their brain; thus, Noah would have had 100 percent brain cell activity. In essence, this information was taught to me when I was a teenager but as we all know, in this age of information we live in, these statistics can change or be sort of rocky. And I am sure doctors and scientists, such as the late Albert Einstein, was a great asset for America in the 1940s. But my Bible tells me that the man Christ Jesus is still greater than any person in history; Christ is the one who has given us the knowledge we do possess and the ability to learn. We can find satisfaction in knowing He is in control of "everyday people," both us and Mr. Albert Einstein no matter how great they may be in the eyes of humankind.

Beyond the talk of knowledge and how much we know as humans, my prayer for you is that you will walk in the peace of God vehemently, like never before, causing the angels of the Lord to work on your behalf to bring prosperity, hope, deliverance, and healing into your life and family; I declare it right now in the name of Jesus! *"Beloved, I pray that you may prosper in all things and be in health, just as your soul prospers"* (3 John 1:2 NKJV).

This doctrine we put our faith in, with the people of God, sounds immense to many people. But truly it is very simple; we must just follow the first principle in order to maintain the blessings of God, and that is walking in the fear of the Lord. Jesus said, *"But seek first the kingdom of God and His righteousness, and all these things shall be added to you"* (Matt. 6:33 NKJV).

HONOR YOUR FATHER AND MOTHER

Obeying our parents with reverential fear does not spring from a horrific or devilish fear, but a deferential fear that we release out of high respect for our mother and father. We must recognize their authority over us with hearts flooded with honor toward them. God commands us, *"Honor your father and your mother, that your days may be long upon the land which the Lord your God is giving you"* (Exod. 20:12 NKJV).

Thinking about my own mother helps me to realize and appreciate all that she had to put up with. She knew giving birth to me at a young age was a choice she had to really ponder, considering the position she was already in. She had the choice to have me aborted, knowing full well her days were going to be very hard and strenuous. Residing in Brooklyn, in the toughest neighborhoods of New York City, was not a walk in the park for her. I give my mother the utmost respect for choosing life. Although, I am climbing into my upper 30s, I still praise God for the choice she made to keep me; otherwise this vision God has given me would have never come into being.

She has moments when she still treats me as if I was a little kid. I know now it's because she really loves me, and in her eyes, I will always be her little boy. But in my earlier years, I had a problem with feeling like her little boy. But I have learned to humble myself, since she has the right to feel and see me in that way. My pride wouldn't let me see the love of a mother to a son until I had children of my own. If I had known then what I know now, I would not have talked with so much disrespect to my mother. Sharply, I would respond, saying, "I am a man. Stop treating me like a little kid. You can't talk to me that way!"

In my mind, something so small and obscure seemed so big to me; understanding was not resonating in my heart. Issues like this were such a big deal to me, and yet so small to everyone else. I was constantly overreacting about small matters, telling my friends, "My mother shouldn't treat me like that because I am a man. I'm not a little kid anymore." Indeed, this attitude I had was the mind of a child. Being shrewd with my mother was my middle name, instead of just following God's commandment to honor her while living under her roof. In my heart, I wanted her to compensate me for all the wrong things she had done. A door of rebellion was open in my heart, but I did not know what the final result would be. Due to this attitude of witchcraft (First Samuel 15:23 says that rebellion is witchcraft), my actions worsened like she had never seen before.

One day, coming over for dinner, I said some harsh things to my mom, and for the first time in my life, I saw the pain of my mother's heart as she began to cry. That was the first time I really noticed her being broken, and I repented and left her home. I asked myself, *What is the matter with you?* Then I heard a small voice say, "One of these days, your mother will be silent and never speak again until the Last Day, so take advantage of loving her with all you have now while she is still borrowing My Breath of Life." Ever since that experience and my choice to repent before the Lord to stay in the broken place, my relationship with my mother is better. Thank God! I didn't realize then what I realize now. When I heard those words from the Lord, something inside of me exploded and caused me to think for the better.

I encourage you to do the same. Give honor where honor is due. Obey your father and mother so that you will live long on earth; it's a promise.

> *Honor your father and your mother, as the Lord your God has commanded you, that your days may be long, and that it may be well with you in the land which the Lord your God is giving you* (Deuteronomy 5:16 NKJV).

We only have one mother and one father. Honoring them is of utmost importance. Unfortunately, the fathers are not as recognized as the mothers are. God doesn't see male or female, Jew or Gentile, but simply His children whom He loves dearly (see John 16:27; 1 John 4:19). One day our parents will not be here, and we will have to pick up where they left off and become better examples for our children and our children's children as God has already done for us.

Let's give honor where honor is due—to our parent or parents. This also applies to those who don't have their real parents. It makes no difference to the Lord; in His eyes, the people who raise a child are considered parents. We must love them with all the love and compassion we have, showing them how we truly feel toward them. For some of us, it's been awhile, and there are things between us and our parents that are floating above our heads, keeping us from a loving relationship. Life is too short to harbor bitterness or resentment for past mistakes. Here is an example of what I would say to my mother, since my father hasn't been around: *"Mom, you are both my mother and father, and you're my closest friend, confidant, counselor, a well of wisdom, and a powerful woman of God. I love you."*

We must demonstrate our love by honoring our parents, for this is right. No one can take that away from us, ever. Times will come when we will not agree or get along with our parents, but we must keep in the back of our minds that our moms and dads love us and that under it all is concern and care for us. They may not have learned how to express the love you so desired. Or, they may have mistreated you while you were growing up, and perhaps felt in your heart like the black sheep of your own family. Many times we don't know how to express ourselves correctly to make these important emotions known to our parents or parent, whether in agreement pertaining to their behavior how you were treated. Here's a secret; we can agree to disagree. Just because we are right doesn't mean we always have to be. To be honest, it's good to just keep silent sometimes. Your mother or father may never get it even though they may be wrong. It's better to just let things be and allow God to handle it while you keep them in prayer. This way, you can still forgive them in order to be able to move forward; in the end this will not allow any kind of bitterness to take root within your heart—though the issue(s) you had with mom and dad weren't resolved. We must use godly wisdom when it comes to family relationships.

Imagine an adult daughter is at her folks' house and a spat arises; she happens to be right about something, but she says what's right in a wrong and disrespectful way. In the end, this makes her wrong. There were times when my mother and I didn't get along or agree on anything. Years have gone by that I can never get back, years of not speaking to each other, but simply bickering and picking on each other. I honor God, because when the valley of brokenness and calamity left my heart, my relationship with my mother improved drastically.

We must keep in mind the fact that the way we treat our parents is the same admiration, devotion, understanding, fear, and love we have directed to the Holy Spirit of God (whether we realize it or not). Let's take time right now and give thanks to the Lord for all He has done so far in our lives.

Thank You so much Lord for what You have done! There are no words to express what stirs in the depths of my soul.

In summary, we were made to have reverential fear for those in authority. If we learn to fear the Lord, we will have respect and fear toward those who have rule over us, including our parents and Church authorities.

THE BEGINNING OF FEAR

When the discipline of God falls into our spirits, it tends to work completely, leaving no residue behind to allow the same issue to occur again. Months will go by as we wonder where the Lord has been hiding in our trial of adversity. The prophet Isaiah believed that the Lord is a God who needs to be sought after to get results for our adversities (see Isa. 64:7).

Surely I looked for my Savior during all those times of misery and suffering. With my hands wide open, I wondered, *Do I really love God? Am I wise enough to take responsibility as a man of God and cultivate a good character? Do I fear God as I should?* Bombarded with questions, ideas, and images of wonderment, I prayed, telling the Lord, "How can this happen to me? I fear You, but am I doing good in your eyes, Lord?" All along, I was convincing myself, trying to make Jesus see a different side of me. In actuality, I did not fear Him as I should have.

The fear of the Lord puts us in a position that helps us not fall away from God when troubles come. We are reminded that if we do this sinful thing or continue in that error of wickedness, we will perish! I now have total reverent fear toward the Lord. I respect who He is, and I strive for perfection. The Bible tells us that we are to seek perfection and that it will bring a spirit of excellence and completion, baptizing us into maturity and wholeness in His Son (see Jas. 1:4).

Perfect means to be whole, mature, and complete; the world has perverted this word to mean never thinking, saying, or doing anything wrong. This is a wrong understanding. When the Scriptures mention *perfect*, it does not mean infallible; only Christ walked in infallibility (see 2 Cor. 5:21). In essence, we must walk in perfection and faith, believing that there is nothing greater than having eternal life, even though we might go through some trepidation, temptation, heartache, and heavy burdens. The Comforter is always by our side. If we fear the Lord, do what is right in His sight, and never mind the rest, we will live longer (see Prov. 10:27), and Jesus will come to our aid. Here is Jesus' promise for all those who fear the Lord:

> *Come to Me, all you who labor and are heavy laden, and I will give you rest. Take My yoke upon you and learn from Me, for I am gentle and lowly in heart, and you will find rest for your souls. For My yoke is easy and My burden is light* (Matthew 11:28-30 NKJV).

PRAYER FOR THE WISDOM OF FEARING GOD

> *Father I thank You for Your grace and mercy that You have shown me throughout my entire life. I know there isn't a way to pay You back for all You have done for me, but I choose to give my life to You and walk in the realm of obedience. Forgive me if I have done or said anything unknowingly that upset You or dishonored You. I ask you to forgive me, Lord. I realize that the fear of the Lord is*

the wisdom of Christ and is very important for enabling me to abide by Your standards.

> *I pray the Holy Spirit will retrain my mind to understand that I must give You total and true reverence. Help me to be sincere and honest with myself and to come before You with humility and meekness in my spirit. I surrender my will, my ways, to You, my God. Help me as I pray this new petition so that You can be glorified in front of all people. From now on, true worship and true praise will continue to be part of who I am, not just in public, but also in secret, and You will reward me openly. Thank You, Father. I pray this in the name of Your precious Son, Jesus. Amen.*

CHAPTER FOUR

Who Do You Say That I Am?

He said to them, "But who do you say that I am?"
Peter answered and said, "The Christ of God."
—LUKE 9:20 NASB

Many people in the Church need a clearer understanding concerning the five-fold ministry. The other day I met a woman who had no idea what an apostle or a prophet is or what they do for the Body of believers. She had been serving the Lord almost all her life; she was in her 60s, but absolutely clueless. Unfortunately, many believe that apostles and prophets do not exist today. Theologians claim that there were no more apostles after the original 12, who literally walked with Christ on earth and established the Church. One loophole I found in that theory is the fact that Paul, Barnabas, and countless others didn't walk with Christ, yet were considered apostles (see Acts 14:14; Gal. 1:1).

A fair number of people whom I have known throughout the years have tried to dictate to God who we are instead of allowing the Holy Ghost to make that decision. If the Lord has called a person to be a prophet and the Spirit confirms it through His ministers (an apostle, pastor, or some other Church leader), that person should receive and walk in that call—with wisdom. Such a person should go through whatever is needed in order to walk in that anointing under the spiritual guidance of a pastor or spiritual authority.

When people receive a call to the five-fold ministry, it is OK to seek a second or a third confirmation to make sure they are hearing right. But if they start looking for even more confirmation or searching for validation, it becomes a problem and is considered doubt and unbelief. On the other hand, some people hear the call and run with it. They go in search of a robe at their local Christian store, begin to look for a building, and go full-force into the ministry, though they have not yet been sent by the Lord. This too is dangerous. We must keep in mind that even the Great Apostle, Jesus Christ, was pointed out by the chief prophet, John the Baptist (see Heb. 3:1; Luke 7:28). He too had to wait until the Father said when to go and the prophet pointed Him out as the Lamb of God who takes away the world's sin. He was baptized by John, who was preparing the way for the Son of God, in order to fulfill all righteousness. John and Jesus were always led by the Spirit, and they knew exactly what their missions were and who they were in God.

IS IT DISOBEDIENCE?

When a man or woman of God tells an individual, by divine revelation, that God has a specific calling on that person's life, it is disobedience if that person does not receive that Word, but instead doubts God's Word. A choice to not accept the Word of the Lord is the same as doubt and unbelief. Such a person refuses and walks the other way, like Jonah did to Nineveh (see Jon. 1:1-3; Rom. 8:28).

We have to know who we are; satan knows us very well—all of our likes, dislikes, and weaknesses. He will make sure we do not walk in that calling, but rather reject the prophetic Word spoken over us, distorting the truth of who we are in the natural and in the spiritual realm. In the ordinary dimensions of the world, when we don't accept the assignments given to us, satan will raise up "hell agents" and counterfeits to bring all kinds of confusion and turmoil into our lives. This is not from God, *"for God is not the author of confusion but of peace, as in all the churches of the saints"* (1 Cor. 14:33 NKJV).

LET HIM STEAL NO MORE

Jesus asked His disciples, *"Who do you say that I am?"* (Luke 9:20 NKJV). By the power of the Spirit of the Lord, Peter the apostle said, *"You are the Christ, the Son of the living God"* (Matt. 16:16 NKJV). It's very important that we know who we are at all times—and *whose* we are. Subsequently, we will be able to walk in the fullness of God's power without any shadow of a doubt. Knowing who we are will bring such mayhem into the camp of the enemy it will make his head spin.

The devil is a powerful enemy! We must not play with satan under any circumstances. We know that the Spirit of Christ indwells us, but that is no reason to become the Lone Ranger trying to take the devil on alone. It is vital that we actually get this deep down into our spirits and let it stay there. The devil's job is to try to stop us from walking right into our calling. He works to impede us from accepting the whisper of the Lord's voice and to keep us moving in the opposite direction. We don't want to miss our glory. That would be a terrible thing to miss the call God has for our lives; it will make our world shudder.

THE DEVIL'S RUNWAY

Regrettably, a lot of Christians run away from the ministry; in essence, it's God whom they are running from. Some simply just don't care to be part of the work that needs to be done. Jesus said, *"The harvest is plentiful, but the workers are few"* (Luke 10:2). We have to get on the ball before time is up. It's sin if God is calling us into the ministry and we do not pursue it. Disobedience is not the will of God. As the Body of the Lord, we must be mature enough to understand that we need to reconsider the Lord's vision, which is the Harvest of souls.

I have often noticed genuine people of the Lord refuse, while the counterfeits are willing to go forth—especially Jehovah's Witnesses as they travel in twos every single weekend in the early mornings, while many of us are still sleeping. That is quite ironic to me. Believers have the real truth, but are keeping it behind the four walls of our homes and churches. However, the devil is out there in all types of weather, as we see Mormons also walking in twos and preaching a lie; most of them are insistent. If they were like this for Christ Jesus, they would be able to move mountains!

Get a move on, and stop the devil and his hell agents dead in their tracks. Get him off the runway that leads into your spirit! I speak to all evangelists to arise and go forth; you are needed now more than ever! It is *always* God's will for His people to preach and teach the good news to all people, in season and out of season.

BEAUTIFUL, BUT DEADLY

One night around 10:00 P.M., I was in my bedroom watching Christian television, and a famous celebrity preacher was speaking about the Holy Spirit. After the program ended, I shut the light off and went to sleep. It's hard to say when my dream actually began, but unexpectedly, as I slept I saw two paths about 20 feet from me. One path was on my far left, and the other was directly in front of me. The wide road, which was in front of me, had the sun shining high in the sky. The clouds were full, and the heavens were blue and beautiful. Birds were chirping and singing, people were laughing as they leisurely walked on this road, while others were playing. Married couples were having picnics on the grass on each side of this beautiful road.

Strange as this may sound, I noticed from my peripheral vision that the narrow path kept trying to have me re-focus on it, like it was calling me. Oddly, there were a very select few who would walk onto that narrow pathway; most others moved toward the wide road instead. Now this narrow path was very dirty, and unpaved. There were huge weeds, roots, and large leaves like a jungle would have. In my mind, I knew it would take a lot of effort to try to get through that path. It had trees and bushes knitted together that would dull a machete in minutes. I would say it needed a landscape company to come and trim the hedges, because it was really in bad shape. Essentially, the road in front of me was captivating, and I tried to veer my eyes off that narrow path.

As I strolled on the fine-looking path, it turned into gold. Each brick was paved in stunning gold ingots. On each side was beautiful green grass where people were having cookouts and family activities. I looked down the road, and as far as the eye could see, I saw soaring buildings at a great distance, which appeared to be like an Emerald City. I remember other bricks were made out of other kinds of jewels and gems. The brilliance of these specific bricks was distracting me from looking toward the buildings at the end of this great road, from the gold ones.

Unexpectedly, hundreds and then thousands of people started to walk from behind me, covering this wide road I was on, and eventually bumping into me to pass me because they wanted to get to the city. Literally thousands were going nuts, almost knocking others down just to get to those skyscrapers. As the road began to clear, the thought of the narrow path kept popping in and out of my head. I felt like I was missing something, felt a void of emptiness in my spirit.

However, I stopped paying attention to the narrow path because I was distracted by a figure, which appeared on the right side of the road in the distance. As I strolled along, looking around and engaging the beauty with my eyes— seeing families on each end of this road having a good time talking and laughing—this figure became closer and taller at the same time. When this figure came into focus at about 100 feet, I started backing up, but it kept coming closer at a high speed, quickly reaching 50 feet, then 20 feet. *Run for your life!* ran through my head.

It was a burned demon general about 13 feet tall. His flesh was exposed, and his extended hand had flesh falling off his fingers. In a scoffing, impious, and unbelieving manner, he told me to come to him in a dark voice. He said, "Hmph! Come Luis, this is the wide road that leads to the good life; did you notice the other path? The other path is terrible looking; it's not as fine-looking as this one? You will be wasting your time going through all the trouble trying to walk through that extremely narrow path when my road is easy to travel on and so attractive. What do you say, Luuuiiissssss?"

Before I was given the opportunity to answer him, I awoke from the dream. I pondered the spiritual meaning of the dream, and the next morning, Jesus showed me in Scripture the narrow path that leads to life and the few who find it.

> ***Enter by the narrow gate***; *for wide is the gate and* ***broad is the way that leads to destruction***, *and there are many who go in by it. Because narrow is the gate and difficult is the way which leads to life, and there are few who find it* (Matthew 7:13-14 NKJV).

Choosing the narrow path in obedience to His will brings immortality; in contrast, those who walk on the wide road find only death and destruction. We must believe God to help us choose and stay the course on the narrow path that leads to life eternal.

FIGHT TO THE FINISH

Fight the good fight of faith, *lay hold on eternal life,* ***whereunto thou art also called...*** (1 Timothy 6:12).

Sadly, I understand what it is to hear the call of God and then run away from it, because it was to heavy for me at that time. When you have a call of an apostle, all hell turns against you. Demons know the power of the office of apostle. They do everything and anything to stop apostles from coming forth. But I see a mighty river visitation coming, which has been revealed to me by the Holy Ghost. This "mighty river" is the strong outpouring of God's Spirit. Signs, wonders, creative miracles, great healings, and mighty miracles are coming and breaking out everywhere. We are going to witness the supernatural very soon. This "mighty river" is also a great revival-taking place that the church and the world have never seen before. Hallelujah to God Almighty! There is nothing satan can do to you as long as you keep your heart in the hands of the Christ of Heaven. The Spirit of God will empower you like you have never witnessed before.

The Scriptures tell us to stay in constant prayer (see 1 Thess. 5:17). Jesus said we should always pray and never lose heart (see Luke 18:1). This is a major key to fighting the good fight of faith. It's not the position of our bodies, but the position of our hearts that matters. Praying on our knees is a sign of humility, but so is a sincere cry to God for help while standing up. Basically, we can pray anywhere, particularly if we pray from the heart instead of just speaking words in vain from our heads. God is more concerned with heartfelt prayers than mental babble.

In my life, during my time of praying and receiving of the plan God has for me, the devil fought and declared war against me. He antagonized me to the point that I couldn't even think straight until the Lord intervened. It's awful to have an adversary who is unyielding, using his children to come against you, then dealing with you on a moment-to-moment basis. It got so bad that satan literally had to show up. I will share that with you in a later chapter; it was a terrible experience.

KNOW WHO YOU ARE

The Lord asked the disciples, in the Garden of Gethsemane, if they could stay up for one hour to pray (see Matt. 26:40, 41). Many pastors have a very hard time getting lay members and even leaders to meet in the house of God to pray. Spending time with our Daddy to make sure our lives are right in the sight of Heaven is very important for all who are born again. Moses, Jeremiah, Joshua, and Gideon are good examples of the select few I am writing about, regarding their belief in the Lord. Joshua needed to be strong and courageous (see Josh. 1:7); Moses stammered (see Exod. 4:10); Jeremiah feared (see Jer. 1:5-8); Gideon wondered if God was really speaking to him concerning the war he was about to face, desiring for God to be by his side (see Judges 6:36-40).

In these end times, we often get our call confused. We may automatically assume that if sister so-and-so has a word of knowledge, then she is a prophetess. But this is a wrong assumption. Just because people prophesy, it does not make them prophets. God may have used that sister in the prophetic gifting, but that doesn't mean she has the call of a prophet. It could be possible, but we must never assume, because assumption is the cousin of accusation.

It's dangerous to just presume about events in our everyday lives—the spirits of assumption and accusation will begin to cling to us. Falling into these pitfalls of the adversary will cause us to embrace an assuming spirit, interpreting things by the optical lens of assumption, accusation, and gossip. Be attentive of that. This is how the devil plays with our minds. He tries to steal what was spoken to us, to kill the hope we have in our hearts for the call and the Word given in order to destroy our faith. The devil doesn't have the right, authority, or power to steal, kill, and destroy unless we give it to him. Praise God for Jesus!

So when you ask God, "Lord, who do You say that I am?" if He answers with any of the five-fold ministry gifts, accept it. Or if He answers with any other call, you must take it by force relentlessly! *"The kingdom of heaven suffers violence, and the violent take it by force"* (Matt. 11:12 NKJV). God will not force you to do something you don't want to do. He will nudge your spirit. When He sees that you are not budging and are always fighting His Spirit, He will stop. This could be months or even years later. The day will come when He will no longer push you to do what He wills. Once you do say "yes" to walking in your call, do not look back, or you will not be fit for the Kingdom of Heaven (see Luke 9:62).

It takes awhile for the call on your life to actually come to fruition. As time goes on, you will recognize a difference in the natural because of the result of the spiritual, inviting you into a place called the wilderness period. Yes, you wait on the Lord; how you wait is very important. You must always be in an attitude of prayer and obedience. I have mentioned this several times because it is imperative to the hearts and minds of believers.

Are you wondering, "Who does God say I am in the body of believers for the Glory of God?" Maybe confusion has settled in and you needed clarity. *"For God is not the author of confusion but of peace, as in all the churches of the saints"* (1 Cor. 14:33 NKJV). God will remind you over and over again that He will not leave you in the dust. If everything else fails and no one else is there for you when you need them, don't fret; God is always there, especially when you think He left to a distant land. Times of testing will visit you on diverse occasions. Here is a list of Scriptures to encourage and strengthen you when you start feeling weary. Use these passages to build up your faith and strengthen your walk with Christ.

> *Finally, my brethren, be strong in the Lord and in the power of His might* (Ephesians 6:10 NKJV).

> *..."Not by might nor by power, but by My Spirit," says the Lord of hosts* (Zechariah 4:6 NKJV).

> *...Do not be afraid nor dismayed because of this great multitude, for the battle is not yours, but God's* (2 chronicles 20:15 NKJV).

> *The Lord shall fight for you, and ye shall hold your peace* (Exodus 14:14).

> *It is of the Lord's mercies that we are not consumed, because His compassions fail not. They are new every morning: great is Thy faithfulness.*

The Lord is my portion, saith my soul; therefore will I hope in Him. The Lord is good unto them that wait for Him, to the soul that seeketh Him (Lamentations 3:22-25).

WHO AM I?

It took me awhile to accept who I am in the eyes of the Lord. He told me in 2002 that I am His apostle. I didn't know what apostles do nor did I believe they existed. Who am I to argue with God and say He is wrong? God then confirmed it down the road through a couple of evangelists; it was like they knew my life. That was the seventh time God said specific and timely prophetic words to me through people I did not know. We were invited one evening by a good friend of mine to visit a church for a five-day revival. Later on that night, my wife got excited to go worship God with other believers at this church down the road from our home. There was a dynamic and anointed speaker by the name of Evangelist Donna, who was speaking that night. As the service was drawing to a close, she came straight toward us and said under the anointing, "Sir you and your wife are called to be an apostle and a prophetess to the nations since your mothers' wombs." On and on she went; it was like she knew us personally. The Holy Spirit was very specific this time around. (In order to get to the new level, we had to step on the old devil).

Providentially, about three weeks later, we were invited to another meeting. This time it was to see Evangelist Ted Shuttlesworth, who was associated with the late Mr. R.W. Shambach, a true weapon of God. My wife didn't understand why I was so excited. Little did my wife know

I watched Evangelist Ted Shuttlesworth on his program *Faith Alive* on Trinity Broadcasting Network (TBN). So my wife and I woke up early to get ready for church. While she was in the bedroom, I entered into the bathroom and prayed to the Lord for guidance and clarity. I had been hearing so many voices around me regarding who I am and what I am not; it kind of left me up in the air. Before I walked out of the bathroom, I asked the Holy Spirit to confirm this "big call" to go preach the Gospel to the nations of the earth. Personally, that is a big call to handle. But God is a big God, and He answered my prayer for confirmation.

On June 28, 2009, during the service, a pastor gave us the order of service about Evangelist Ted Shuttlesworth coming from out of town to speak that morning—and every night for the next six days. We were so excited and couldn't wait for the service to begin. When it finally began, the anointing was very heavy. The anointing of God was so strong I didn't realize Evangelist Ted Shuttlesworth was walking toward us. To our surprise, he called us up to stand in front of about 1,200 witnesses. God confirmed and validated my wife and I in front of everyone who doubted us and those who did not believe we were righteous and holy in the sight of God. Evangelist Ted Shuttlesworth had this service set up to play again later on the Internet and also on his program on TBN, *Faith Alive.* Under the power of the anointing Evangelist Ted Shuttlesworth gave us a Word from the Lord, confirming every detail that was said to us weeks and months before by other believers who walk in the five-fold ministry.

O YE OF LITTLE FAITH

Prior to all of this, I had a reason not to believe and had ended up in a state of confusion. Since lay people, pastors, and other ministers we knew had started claiming apostles do not exist today, my faith was declining. They were even claiming that my wife and I are not real believers. Even my own family didn't believe me, saying, "I don't know about this Luis; you really need to pray, go to church, and wait and see where in the ministry God needs you. Go sit under a pastor and let him guide you." But the Lord told me that I am not to be under a pastor; pastors are to be under me. He told me that at the church that I would build we would set up staff and then ascertain church government in its proper format. It blew my mind!

Today the fulfillment of God and His Word is becoming stronger and more evident as the days go by. Many didn't and still do not understand the call of an apostle because no one is teaching who we are and what we can do in this age. Nevertheless, I have been waiting on God for over 10 years; when I first heard the call, I hid! He has been calling me, and I kept dodging Him, so He announced my call in front of everyone so there wouldn't be a reason for me to be in hiding. (I tell you, God will find you; wherever you go, it makes no difference to Him. Praise God for Jesus!) All the counterfeits and the hypocrites had started declaring that I didn't know what I was talking about, saying that kind of call is not true. This is a prime example of the importance of thinking twice about who you share your visions with. Families sometimes can be worse than friends. Sadly, sometimes you will find more grace and mercy from the mouths of sinners than Christians! Some Christians will eat you alive!

Thankfully, no matter what others were saying, God was not giving up on me. Instead, He pursued me just as the psalmist described:

> *Where can I go from Your Spirit? Or where can I flee from Your presence? If I ascend into heaven, You are there; if I make my bed in hell, behold, You are there. If I take the wings of the morning, and dwell in the uttermost parts of the sea, even there Your hand shall lead me; and Your right hand shall hold me* (Psalm 139:7-10 NKJV).

When I was being verbally attacked, I stated, "The call was not from people, but from the Holy Spirit of God!" There wasn't much to say after that; some have held their peace.

No matter what your call or how much fruit you see in your ministry, you will still have those who will not believe the ministry the Lord has for you. Nevertheless, you must go forth and do what God has commissioned you to do in spite of what people say. You must continue to believe God and press forward in all that you do for Him. Now, I know who I am in the Lord, and no one can take that away from me, but me. When God opens a door, no person can ever close it (see John 10:7). Paul understood this when he wrote about his call, *"For I neither received it from man, nor was I taught it, but it came through the revelation of Jesus Christ"* (Gal. 1:12 NKJV).

When I heard the voice of the Holy Ghost, when He jolted my spirit and told me that I am His apostle, God had to remind me over and over again that He simply loves me. He said this to me one day—it meant so much to me.

"If you don't feel like anyone loves you, know that I love you." Those words resonated in my heart. He knew what I was thinking before I even thought it. He is so awesome, especially when He speaks to me. Once I knew the call and accepted it, it was like all hell broke loose in my life.

CALL? WHAT CALL?

I knew a pastor once who was called to be an apostle through various prophets and evangelists who would visit the church, confirming what was spoken to him before. In his disobedience, he rejected *the call* because he was going through too much distress and chaos as a pastor. He told me in his church one day, "Imagine if I accept the call of apostle, man; more demons and more problems will come my way." What he failed to recognize is that the higher we are in the anointing of the Spirit, the more power we will have to endure to fight satan's devils, warlocks, evil legions, witches, and every other realm of darkness that opposes us.

We must not let fear, doubt, or an unbelieving heart—as was plainly the case with this pastor—overtake us, or we will not prosper. It can stop the flow of the Holy Ghost from coming in to move in the way He really wants to in our lives. A contorted spirit of bitterness and unforgiveness can settle in. This has become the case with this man toward me for sharing the Word, but the forgiveness I illustrated to him was much greater, even though he has rejected me. We must demonstrate love at a higher level and be the mature ones who are willing to fall on the lap of the Ancient of Days, loving anyone under His power and anointing. As I have walked my path, I have encountered my share of men who deny who I really am, sometimes causing me to struggle all the more to accept who God called me to be, but in all my years, I've never let it stop me from pressing toward the mark that is set before me. I will fulfill my destiny!

Accepting the fact that God still loved me after all my mess-ups, I pressed on. I had been abandoned by people and subjected to various kinds of hurt, pain, misery, and failure. The operative word for me was *failure*. I felt like a failure as a son, a business owner, a man, a father, and a husband—never really accomplishing anything worth conversing about. It cut me down to the very core, with no one to my left or my right to build me up, enlighten me, or encourage me.

We must realize that God will never deal with us the way He deals with others. He trains us each uniquely. Learning the hard way and going forward on my own with the Almighty was all that I needed, but not everyone is dealt the same cards that were handed to me. The Holy Spirit taught me and called me, not other people—similar to the apostle Paul:

> *But I make known to you, brethren, that the gospel which was preached by me is not according to man. For I neither received it from man, nor was I taught it, but it came through the revelation of Jesus Christ* (Galatians 1:11-12 NKJV).

I would go to church service, and when I attended, it really took a lot out of me because several times I would know things about the end-time church years in advance. Different visions and revelation of the future would show up before my eyes while the pastor is speaking. Further, some leaders, teachers, pastors, and regular churchgoers would not understand my calling and the revelations given to me by the Lord.

There will be people whom you are able to reach that a different person can't and vice versa. Winning souls is the name of the game. God really loves and adores you; male or female, Jew or Gentile, it makes no difference to God. On a greater level, He can change you, whether you are a murderer, a thief, or a sex offender; if you are guilty of any of these, with the added hurt and pain of having been ostracized, exploited, and gossiped about, God will accept you when you come to Him with a repented heart and a humble spirit. Society will treat you irrationally and call you a monster (indeed, the act against the victim is evil!), but God will turn it around and call you blessed, highly favored, and a new creation. He will heal both the violator and the victim, especially those who come to Him in penitence for their wicked ways.

He will heal the victim to a higher degree than you can ever imagine. If you are a victim, you must turn to Him and forgive others and yourself for the act you did not invite and forgive those who caused it. God called several men and women in the Scripture who were worse off than us, and He used them for His glory. The Lord always runs after the unwanted, the unsuccessful, the beaten, the raped, the molested, the unattractive, the rejected, and He molds them into fine gold of great value. He uses the brokenhearted, the hated, the forgotten, the uneducated, the lost, and the hungry—as well as the rich, the educated, and the successful. The Eyes of Compassion desire to use anyone, whether in low or high positions in life.

What I've noticed is God's way of breaking people. He loves to use broken people for His glory. Weakness in His sight is strong; the lowly and the humble will bear engaging fruit in the sight of others with no problem because they will be prepared to walk in God's strength. In order for us to know who we are, we have to have Jesus' Spirit living on the inside of us. Knowing our true selves and finding our position of purpose in the Lord will always give us the upper hand.

People play games constantly with the grace that has been given freely; my question is, "Are we to carry on in foolishness and mock His holiness?" The Scriptures say that God cannot be mocked and that what we sow we shall also reap (see Gal. 6:7). We must be very careful. We can amuse ourselves with certain things without becoming an obstacle to ourselves and those around us as long as we take seriously the things of our Creator and keep our amusements in their rightful place. This is the real deal! If we want to know who we are, we must give our lives to Christ and stay with Christ. Then, and only then, will we find our identity. He is the only truth that exists on the earth; there is no other (see John 14:6).

We must always be in a mode to say *yes* to God when He needs us. We will not regret it. I hear people all the time say that we are not worthy. I know what they mean fundamentally. But if we were not worth it, Jesus would have never come down to die for us, and God would not have sent Him in the first place. He will never tell us to do something to hurt or destroy us. He loves us too much to lose His relationship with us after spending years wooing us to Himself. The only thing that can destroy us is if we choose to blaspheme His Holy Spirit (see Matt. 12:31-32).

If we did it out of ignorance while we were in the world, it is different. But if we know full well about the Lord and His Word and we blaspheme His Spirit, the high price we will have to pay will stagger us—our lives will be over, even while we live.

Dealing with sanctified people who fall into these various pits and trying to keep them in right standing with Jesus is complex on occasion. Ministry can be tough, and it is often very strenuous working for God and His people. I am sure all those in ministry would agree with me. We understand why Moses initially acted out in anger and stress—tens of thousands of people were coming to him with their complaints and grumbling (see Exod. 16:7). To put it in perspective, regarding the ministry and the Spirit of God, as we deal with the children of the Most High we must make sure we do not walk in rebellion and blaspheme the Spirit, who is doing the work. To those who blaspheme knowingly, I say they should live their lives to the fullest, because they will not be forgiven in this world or in the world to come. Imagine what that is, to be never forgiven for all eternity—it's a life full of anger, hopelessness, and utter disaster and a future of lost dreams and eternal anguish, bathed in fire!

> *Wherefore I say unto you, all manner of sin and blasphemy shall be forgiven unto men: but **the blasphemy against the Holy Ghost shall not be forgiven unto men**. And whosoever speaketh a word against the Son of man, it shall be forgiven him: but whosoever speaketh against the Holy Ghost, it shall not be forgiven him, neither in this world, neither in the world to come* (Matthew 12:31-32).

As you learn how to deter negative people and wicked spirits through people, you have to reach for Christ with all you have. You do not have time to wait for someone else to tell you who you are. Ask Christ the Lord with boldness and confidence, "Lord, who do You say that I am?" Expect an answer. I guarantee you, without a shadow of a doubt, He will tell you. If His Divine Seed, which is the Holy Spirit, decreases in your heart, you will never make it to the wedding table in His holy Heaven. Take dominion for what is right with the intention to put your mess into proper alignment; the Lord will bless you beyond measure for your efforts.

PRAYER

Father, thank you so much for sending your Son to earth so I may have life. I am who I am in You, because You chose to come from Heaven to die for me. In doing so, that enabled me to be able to know my true identity in You. So many don't understand who they are or what it means to be a born- again Christian. Give me the words and strength to help those to know what it means to give their lives over to You, and become true Christians who would actually love You. And I also pray that you continue to give me the understanding of what it means to be an original and not a counterfeit. Desiring to be truthful always no matter my circumstance is my goal. Ultimately my hope is in You. It is such a blessing, Father, that you are able to make things work for my good. I have no clue how to get out of a bad situation. Surely, You are my "everything" when life goes off balance. Thank you Lord for loving me and hearing my prayer. In the name of Jesus I pray. Amen.

CHAPTER FIVE

The Cross and the Conqueror

Yet in all these things we are more than conquerors through Him who loved us.

*—*ROMANS 8:37 NASB

For the message of the cross is foolishness to those who are perishing, but to us who are being saved it is the power of God.

*—*1 CORINTHIANS 1:18 NASB

The cross of Christ is a very powerful symbol, which represents the nature of God's "big idea"—how He used it to defeat His enemies: satan, death, and sin. The preaching of the cross is foolishness to those perishing because of the natural person. While I'm on the subject of the cross, let me share a symbol with you, which will look very familiar.

THIS IS NOT A "PEACE" SIGN

Poignant as it seems, I have seen hundreds, if not thousands, of born-again Christians in this country and around the world with this symbol around their necks, on their belts, and on their clothing. Scores of others have tattooed this pagan symbol on themselves without realizing what it actually means. It's true what Hosea the prophet said in the Scriptures, affirming that God's people are destroyed for a lack of knowledge, an absence of important information (see Hos. 4:6). This pagan symbol, with the cross of Christ upside down and the arms broken downward literally means: *Christianity is defeated and the work done on the Cross is ailing!*

Throughout the last 2,000 years, this symbol has designated hatred of Christians. History says, Nero, who loathed Christians and who was part of the ten persecutions[1] in the past, had the apostle Peter crucified on a cross upside down. This repugnant event resembled the Teutonic (Germanic) cross and became a popular pagan emblem of their day. Thereafter, this symbol became recognized as the Neronic cross. The peace symbol is also called and known as the:

- *Broken Cross*

- Crow's Foot

- Christianity is defeated

- Witch's Foot

- Nero's Cross

- Sign of the Broken Jew

- Symbol of the antichrist

- Gesture of despair

- Death of humankind

"The so-called peace symbol[2] is used by satanists to worship satan. The V shape in the inside has been glorified by the founder of satan's church, Anton S. LaVey.[3] The V sign has a multihued history. V is the sign of the Romans for the number five. Dr. Adam Weishaupt founded the Illuminati on May 1, 1776.[4] He was the professor of Cannon Law at the University of Ingolstadt, Bavaria, Germany, and he used the symbol for his Illuminati to signify the "Law of Fives."

In the Kabbalah/Cabala, the Hebrew letter V for Van is Nail. Within the brotherhood of satanism, the Nail is one of the secret titles of satan. He also uses the pentagram (a five-pointed star), and the five-fold salute is used in Masonry and witchcraft."

Hopefully this makes us rethink throwing up the "peace sign" with our hands. Having this information stored in the back of our minds will keep us in the safe zone with God and protect us from the iniquitous campaigns of "the man of lawlessness" (see 2 Thess. 2:3 ESV). In the same course, as we strive and go full speed ahead with vigor in our commitments to the Lord, we will come to a place of understanding our motives and attitudes regarding how we think and speak with our own souls.

The soul contains our will, emotions, and intellect. To simplify it, here are four kinds of people in the world—the carnal person, the natural person, the spiritual person, and the two-fold person.

- *Carnal Person* (the flesh)—has the five senses, which makes us world-conscious for a four-dimensional world (taste, touch/feeling, smell, hear, sight, and time).

- *Natural Person* (the soul)—makes us self-conscious, gives us awareness and intelligence.

- *Spiritual Person* (the spirit)—makes us God conscious, able to perceive the divine things of God.

- *Two-fold Person* (the flesh and soul)—waivers on a constant basis, unstable in every way—sometimes devilish.

Carnal-minded people don't believe Heaven, hell, God, or the devil exist. They live with the philosophy, if I can see it or touch it, I believe it. They are persuaded to accept many things because there are no absolutes (see Ps. 14:1; 53:1).

Natural-minded people believe that whether there is a God or a devil makes no difference. They say, "You believe what you believe, and I will believe what I want to believe." Their consciences have been seared as with a hot iron, and they think a man dying on a cross is foolishness (see 1 Cor. 1:18; 1 Tim. 4:2).

Spiritual-minded people believe everything pertaining to the Scriptures and have the ability to distinguish the divine from the counterfeit. The cross of Christ, in their minds, *is* the power of God. They know they need God in all circumstances for they have been crucified with Christ, and they no longer live (see 1 Cor. 1:18; Gal. 2:20).

Double-minded or *two-fold* people vacillate between faith and unbelief. They may believe the truth, but then a "care of this life" arrives, and they end up losing heart. In one moment, they believe God to fix their situation; the next day, they believe in themselves to fix the same situation. One day they have faith; the next minute they are doubtful, question-bound, and full of worry and fear. Living an oscillating lifestyle, they swing through the pendulum of speech, fixated on everyone else's feeble faith while ignoring their own wavering minds. About such people, the Bible says:

> *But let him ask in faith, with no doubting, for he who doubts is like a wave of the sea driven and tossed by the wind. For let not that man suppose that he will receive anything from the Lord; he is a double-minded man, unstable in all his ways* (James 1:6-8 NKJV).

> *Draw near to God and He will draw near to you. Cleanse your hands, you sinners; and purify your hearts, **you double-minded*** (James 4:8 NKJV).

> *Never worry about anything. But in every situation let God know what you need in prayers and requests while giving thanks. Then God's peace, which goes beyond anything we can imagine, will*

guard your thoughts and emotions through Christ Jesus (Philippians 4:6-7 GW).

Since we are comprised as a triune person (body, soul, and spirit) like the Lord, we are always in search of something higher than ourselves. God has programmed us to worship Him in spirit and in truth. Basically, we are speaking spirits who have souls and live in bodies. This is basic Christianity 101. Anyone who holds fast to the Lord must make sure they are in the spiritual-minded person category.

When I attended college, a few professors would teach that human beings do not have a soul. I also heard another professor say that we don't have a spirit. In recent studies and scientific research, I have found something very interesting and relevant to humans having a soul. Remarkably, morticians and scientists put this to the test to see if the body does have a soul within. Sadly, this institution had a handful of people who were nearing their last breath; they lay these ones on a weight scale divan until they passed. When they did pass, every single one of their bodies became 6 pounds lighter. I thought that was interesting since God associates people with the number six throughout the Scriptures (see Gen. 1:26). In addition, it was interesting to know that our soul weighs 6 pounds. However, this has been known as assumptive information and not proven.

YOUR PERSONALITY

In my research, I have found that there are 16 major personalities, but I only mention four below: Phlegmatic,

Choleric, Melancholy, and Sanguine. They all have their own character traits. Others can operate in a mixture of all of them.

- *Phlegmatic*—unemotional, indifferent, composed, slow-moving

- *Choleric*—expresses strong emotion, passionate, easily angered, short-tempered

- *Melancholy*—gloomy, down and depressed, pessimistic

- *Sanguine*—cheerful, loud, confident, optimistic, excited, full of energy

Which personality do you have? It may not be any of them, but you're probably close to one of them.

Personality is only associated with the soul realm. We get caught up in the flesh so much we tend to forget the things we do and say, so as to protrude from the center of our souls. The excuse is, "That's just the way I am; that is my personality. I was born like this, so if you love me, then you need to accept me for who I am." I have good news; we don't have to choose that kind of attitude. It actually falls in line with a spirit of Jezebel, so we must release, repent, rebuke, and be restored, for the devil is a liar! We don't have to become a product of our circumstances or who our parents are or were or even our upbringing. There are no barriers with God.

We must be transformed by the renewing of our minds (see Rom. 12:2). It's the soul that gets renewed, not the spirit. Let's reach out our hands toward the heavens and let the Father of lights hold us once again, whether we are backsliders, believers, or sinners. He loves us just where we are! We don't go to church because our lives are together. We go to church for the reason that our lives are jacked up with so many different everyday issues—we need the sitting Savior. He sits at the right-hand side of God (see Heb. 8:1). This means His work has been fully completed.

NEVER GIVE UP ON YOUR RELATIONSHIP

Do you desire to sit sometimes? I am sure you do. Men, you need rest from the weariness of the world's pressures and learn to spend time loving your wife and family. Find time to hold them all over again, like you have done so many times before. Women, you need to reflect once again to refresh yourselves with the "human well," the Lord Jesus, if your passions are not burning in you the way they used to. Singles and the married alike will face challenges that can sometimes destroy what is really stirring in their hearts. I have met a decent amount of folks who were willing to work their way into a frenzy of illicit behavior of all sorts, to numb the pain of what is going on within them, desiring to give up on relationships that have gone sour.

We must consider ourselves as conquerors! We serve a big God! No problem we or the world system could create will ever be greater than our God. Giving up is not an option; we must embrace what was handed down to us encircled by the people we love. We can encounter a new thing with Him and think twice about our marriages. I pray in the name of Almighty Jesus that He would come and rekindle the flame that once blazed in the ocean of our heart.

I am familiar of the issues that surround your emotions and intelligence; I've been there. I was married, but I didn't have a marriage. Learning how to have one was a long process, but in the end, it was worth it. Jesus is the answer to convince, display, and bring new wine into your old wineskins. He will never give up on you! Not ever! He did it for my wife and me, and we are no better than you. He restored us to His fullness in Him, and He continues to do so to this day. He is the "volume" for your song, the "speaker" for your frequency, the "wind which carries His voice" into parabolic phrases of His great power! Here is the formula for healing and breakthrough: Learn to trust God and lean on His understanding, for His mercy endures forever (see Prov. 3:5-6).

FOLLOW THE LEADER

Now with this holy understanding of who Christ is, we must worship God in spirit, which is our inner, born-again self that has been renewed by salvation (see Rom. 10: 9-10; John 4:24). In order for us to reach God and walk in the power and might of the Lord of Hosts, we must not shy away from correction or the conviction of the Holy Spirit within us. If we do ignore the prompting of the Spirit of God when we sin, we will slowly fall away. Jude 24 declares, *"Now unto Him is able to keep you from falling...."* We are not invincible. The views given by the New Testament writers were very clear; it is possible for us to fall, but the Lord is there to help us back up if we heed His voice (see Rom. 14:4; Jude 1:24). Following the leading of the Holy Spirit is a necessity in our lives if we want to walk with Christ daily.

He is the one who will allow the cross to enter into our minds and penetrate our hearts.

The time has come for us to fall into the hands of the cross. The Almighty Christ has all the supremacy and authority to save the souls of hurting men and women, the young and the old, the lost all around the world. I would rather be a fool speaking one line of truth then speak ten thousand words of pure emptiness. Souls are my main objective. I am writing and speaking to make sure we all have the opportunity to make a decision to accept Christ, especially those of us who are not saved. Essentially, I teach and preach to the saved to keep them saved and to the lost to lead them to salvation.

Our passion should convert into a tireless compassion, enabling us to target everyone and anyone who walks with the "breath of life" in their bodies as perfect image-bearers of God who need the opportunity to be saved. No color, no race, no creed, or religion should ever stop us! I have tried to read people from Jehovah's Witness, Catholicism, Islam, and Secular Humanism—and many more. None of these religions or their ministers were there for me when I was going through so much hell in my life and needed a way of escape. Jesus our Messiah, the world's "paragraph," the world's "essay," the world's "word-walker," must be heard and boasted about to all flesh—laying the flesh and the soul down in submission before Him, now!

Mass quantities of believers are allowing too much foolishness, sinful desire, scandal, and many other sins that I am too ashamed to even write about. Back in the ancient days of the Old Testament Jerusalem, God would not allow such drama and mayhem to take place in His temple. People had to walk blameless and holy in His sight at all times (see Luke 1:6). We must unite hands and love each other unconditionally. There is not enough love going around in our churches today. In the days of the early apostles, people were saying, "I am from Paul," "Well, I am from Cephas," "Oh yeah, and I am from Apollos" (see 1 Cor. 1:12; 1 Cor. 3:4). This is pure imprudence in the eyes of God, yet we still do this today. "I am from Assemblies of God, and we believe in baptizing in the Father, Son, and Holy Ghost." "Well, I am from Church of God in Christ, and we believe in this." "Well, I am Southern Baptist, and we don't speak in that." And the list goes on and on.

The devil couldn't beat the unified Church; I imagine he devised a scheme to make numerous denominations to cause conflict and division within the Church body. He has actually progressed in that area, because we are at each other's throats—right in front of the Master's face—blasting each other with our doctrines. Pastors are not getting along with other pastors because of various arguments, and their biggest worry is that pastor so-and-so will steal their members. Let's get this straight; no one can steal any one from any one, no more than a man stealing another man's wife. People leave on their own simply because they want to leave, not for the reason of being "stolen." Foolishness such as this is not getting the Body of Christ in order. We have to be ready for the second coming of God's Christ! He destroyed on the cross all of our sins and iniquity; therefore, we must not hold any record of wrongdoings among our brothers and sisters in Christ. We must not compare ourselves to others, become jealous, or allow a spirit of envy to creep into our hearts. Proverbs says to *"guard your heart more than anything else..."* (Prov. 4:23 GW). Paul gave us this example,

For we dare not class ourselves or compare ourselves with those who commend themselves. But they, measuring themselves by themselves, and comparing themselves among themselves, are not wise (2 Corinthians 10:12 NKJV).

The cross is the amazement of God's miraculous love and true care for His creation. In times before, we were people without hope and no God in the world. Our world of sin collided with the world of purity, but never came to a suitable union, until Jesus died, bringing it all together into one. We as a people, a Body, must come into agreement with the Lord and make sure His will is done in and for our lives and the lives of others.

MORE THAN CONQUERORS

The conquerors are those who are born from above with His Spirit breathing and living within: *"Yet in all these things we are more than conquerors through Him who loved us"* (Rom. 8:37 NKJV). The Bible says that we are *more* than conquerors, not just conquerors. We need to thank God for this privilege!

The apostle Paul confers his persuasion regarding God's love, knowing this also; it is God's will for us as His children to conquer people with love. Unfortunately, in these last days, we have a big problem demonstrating love to our fellow believers and to our enemies. Where is the love of Christ? Yes—it seems difficult at times, but when we have relationship with our Master, He helps us with His Spirit if we yield, as these Scripture passages demonstrate:

And walk in love, as Christ also has loved us and given Himself for an offering, a sacrifice and us to God for a sweet-smelling aroma (Ephesians 5:2 NKJV).

Which has come to you, as it has also in the entire world, and is bringing forth fruit, as it is also among you since the day you heard and knew the grace of God in truth... (Colossians 1:6 NKJV).

But I say to you, love your enemies, bless those who curse you, do good to those who hate you, and pray for those who spitefully use you and persecute you, that you may be sons of your Father in heaven; for He makes His sun rise on the evil and on the good, and sends rain on the just and on the unjust... (Matthew 5:44-45 NKJV).

We must illustrate love, being holy and pure in His sight and in the sight of people. One way of putting that into practice is by driving back from our wants and preventing ourselves from being placed in a position that would cause us to fall into sin; this is the duty of every believer. We all at some point repent from the sin we've committed, but we are not to stay there. We have to think, speak, and *be* conquerors! We do not *act* like conquerors; it will only be just that—acting. If we keep toddling in this disposition, we will only become actors or performers instead of men and women of God who are truly walking in total holiness and compliance. The Bible states, *"...If God is for us, who can be against us?"* (Rom. 8:31 NKJV) and *"For as many as are led by the Spirit of God, these are sons of God"* (Rom. 8:14 NKJV).

We are not obscure, indistinct, dark, faint, or remote. All things in human life relate to God in some way, shape, or form. We, as the Body of Christ corporately and as individuals, are His alone. We are important. He needs His warriors out there leading unbelievers to Christ, setting a path to uprightness, sanctity, and tranquility. We cannot give up on ourselves or other people so easily. Compassion and love are the essence of the heart of God. We must hold and hug those who find it unfamiliar with the willingness to receive such fervor.

The Word of God does not come back to Him void, but will accomplish all that God has spoken (see Isa. 55:11). It's the same thing when we prophesy into people's lives. We are not to say anything to others that will discourage them, knowing that we reap what we sow (see Gal. 6:7). We must make things right, right now. It is unfortunate to have members backbiting and relying on false words and creative thoughts to speak into the minds of other Christians. If we have something against a brother or sister, we must leave our gifts at the altar and go reconcile. When we have reconciled with our brothers and sisters, we will be able to have clean hearts in the eyes of God to present our gifts to Him (see Matt. 5:23, 24). Building each other up is God's will. We must never think we are in the business to tear down and demolish one another. As believers, we are never to neglect our own. Our job is to bring comfort and encouragement. Here are the four E's, which are the duties of every image-bearer:

- *Exhortation*—to urge and advise strongly

- *Edification*—to improve the moral character or mind of a person.

- *Encouragement*—to inspire with confidence and hope

- *Empathy*—to participate in understanding the feelings or ideas of another

THE BACKSLIDERS

God is married to the backslider, as Jeremiah the prophet so eloquently put it (see Jer. 3:14). If we keep reading the major prophet's writings, we see that it states that if people don't repent, they will not make it into Heaven (see Jer. 4:4). As harsh as it sounds, it is the Word of the Lord. As a watchman, who is a prophet, I must warn God's people. Standing for truth and endurance in the Spirit is the heart of a watchman. Ezekiel described the duty of a watchman:

> *When I say to the wicked, "You shall surely die," and you give him no warning, nor speak to warn the wicked from his wicked way, to save his life, that same wicked man shall die in his iniquity; but his blood I will require at your hand. Yet, if you warn the wicked, and he does not turn from his wickedness, nor from his wicked way, he shall die in his iniquity; but you have delivered your soul. Again, when a righteous man turns from his righteousness and commits iniquity, and I lay a stumbling block before him, he shall die; because you did not give him warning, he shall die in his sin, and his righteousness, which he has done, shall not be remembered; but his blood I will require*

at your hand. Nevertheless if you warn the righteous man that the righteous should not sin, and he does not sin, he shall surely live because he took warning; also you will have delivered your soul (Ezekiel 3:18-21 NKJV).

If the watchman sees the sword coming and does not blow the trumpet, and the people are not warned, and the sword comes and takes any person from among them, he is taken away in his iniquity; but his blood I will require at the watchman's hand...When I say to the wicked, "O wicked man, you shall surely die!" and you do not speak to warn the wicked from his way, that wicked man shall die in his iniquity; but his blood I will require at your hand. Nevertheless if you warn the wicked to turn from his way, and he does not turn from his way, he shall die in his iniquity; but you have delivered your soul (Ezekiel 33:6,8-9 NKJV).

We must do extraordinary things for the Lord like we have never done before. We must visit the sick and pray with them so they too can be healed (see Mark 16:18; Jas. 5:14). We must give, and it will be given back to us (see Luke 6:38). Whether we give loving-kindness or money, or even allow another person to borrow our lives (so to speak) for their time—our Maker will take us to a higher level if we are serving others with the right motives. As channels of God, we are to assist those in need, which in turn brings exaltation.

Give, and it will be given to you: good measure, pressed down, shaken together, and running over will be put into your bosom. For with the same measure that you use, it will be measured back to you (Luke 6:38 NKJV).

SEIZE YOUR LEGACY

Seizing proper significance, as conquering Christians who intermingle our character close to the cross, will lay a foundation for a legacy beyond the limits of this world, both in the spirit as well as in the natural. Paul did the exact same thing and sent the message all across the known planet, having an impact of hope, with anticipation in his soul of seeing the Lord again. Jesus came to give life and to give it to the fullest without us ever being able to lose it (see John 10:10). Our lives will be redefined to the highest degree in the thoughts of those around us—they will begin to see the fruit of Christ's life within us. A legacy of a winning attitude, a contrite spirit, and the essence of tranquility and poise will elevate you to another level in Christ Jesus for the glory of God the Father!

> *I have been crucified with Christ; it is no longer I who live, but Christ lives in me; and the life, which I now live in the flesh I live by faith in the Son of God, who loved me and gave Himself for me* (Galatians 2:20 NKJV).

PRAYER

Strong Father, my life will always mean something within your eyes. There is no one in this world that can truly help me to conquer my fears or anything else that may rise unexpectedly and come my way. I am eternally grateful my Lord that you have come to give me life and wisdom to assist me in my times of need. Forgive me when I don't recognize that You are there by my side. You did say in your Word that You will never leave or abandon me. Help me to always lean on you when things seem to be hectic and don't make any sense at all. Increase my faith Holy Spirit. Help me also to lean on You when good things are happening as well, not just when things are bad. Give me the understanding to know and accept the reality that I as your child must receive in this life the good with the bad. I need You Father. You are the only One in all creation that can make sense out of situations that don't have any sense at all! You are my Rock that I stand on, always. And if I don't stand on You and Your precious Word when required, I ask your forgiveness, and to have mercy on me so I could stand when expected of me. Thank you my Lord and God for hearing my prayer. In Jesus' name. Amen.

ENDNOTES

1. http://www.bibleprobe.com

2. http://www.crossroad.to/books/symbols1

4. http://www.religiouscounterfeits.org

3. http://www.jesus-is-savior.com/falsereligions

CHAPTER SIX

In Spirit and In Truth

But the hour is coming, and now is, when the true worshipers will worship the Father in spirit and truth, for the Father is seeking such to worship Him.

—JOHN 4:23 NKJV

When we pray in the Spirit, in our heavenly language, demons do not understand because we are speaking mysteries to God. Psalm 150:6 states, *"Let everything that has breath, Praise the Lord...."* How can people praise the Lord, exactly? Well, they can praise the Lord in their own language by using God's universal tongue. I know many believers do not believe that speaking in tongues is for today, but they speak in a tongue, nevertheless. Some Bible scholars and leaders from other denominations might not believe in speaking in tongues, declaring it was only for the early church, yet they speak in a tongue. How so?

Hallelu-yah is a universal heavenly language given by God to us, proving that He exists! How do we "Praise the Lord" in God's universal tongue, which is *Halleluyah,* in our own languages? The answer is, *Halleluyah.* In Chinese, it's *Halleluyah!* In English, it's *Halleluyah!* In Afrikaans, it's *Halleluyah!* In German, it's *Halleluyah!* In Thai, it's *Halleluyah!* In French, it's *Halleluyah!* Get the picture?

When we say *Jesus,* in any of these languages, it sounds different.

WHAT'S HIS NAME?

To prove to the Jews that Jesus was truly the Messiah and God in human flesh (see Isa. 7:14; 9:6; 1 Tim. 3:16), I have tried my best to explain how Christ has come in God's name by using the "four letters" Y-H-W-H which you will see as you keep reading. Firstly, we come to know the name of God, "Yahweh," which is a word meaning LORD, and is pronounced with the *Yah* sound in Yahshua or HalleluYah. For some background, those who are not familiar with the Tetragrammaton—the Y-H-W-H rendition of Yahweh—I will lay a small foundation for the "four meaning." Again, the *jah* in *hallelujah* is pronounced like *yah.* I assume publishers began to catch on as we see that in the New King James version, the correct rendering in Psalm 68:4, Isaiah 12:2, Isaiah 26:4, and Isaiah 38:11, from *jah* to *yah*—which is revealed four times in all of the Bible in accordance to the dead sea scrolls. In the name Yahweh we see the letters 'A' and 'E', which denotes the *A* for *Adonai* and the *E* for *Elohim,* because the letter *J* was invented approximately 500 years ago. Most Jews have a problem with the fact we use the 'J' sound for Jesus as opposed to using the 'Y' sound, which is in their alphabet. I had known Jewish people who were very skilled when it came to God's name. They said that the Bible is not clear how Jesus would come in their God's name, which the Scripture at the end of this paragraph states. So I began to explain a little regarding the letter 'J' as you read above and when it was invented to help make sense of the name of Jesus having the J sound and how it comes to play concerning His name. I've stated that the letter *J* and the *J* sound did not exist in the original Hebrew language, and neither did vowels. Hence, Zionists would pronounce *Jesus* as *Yahshua* or *Yeshua,* meaning "salvation saves" (*yah* is "salvation" and *shua* is "saves")— proving Jesus came in His Father's name. *Yahushua* is also a derivative of the name Joshua. *"I have come in My Father's name, and you do not receive Me; if another comes in his own name, him you will receive"* (John 5:43 NKJV). Although I've explained to the best of my knowledge, Jewish associates of mine still rejected the idea of Jesus coming in His God's name. I was using this entire explanation as a witness. Some listened and thought about it while the other Jews rejected the entire ordeal regarding "What's His Name." (As I have spoken to several Jews they shared with me that the letters 'A' and 'E' were added later to protect God's name.)

REALITIES OF THE HEART

He is worthy to be praised, no matter what country, culture, barrier, or background we can think of; God will break the backs of demons and break down any walls that try to counter Him. He will make sure that every praise, prayer, and cry of every spirit who worships Him will reach His ear when it is coming from a heart that is untainted and pious. He is not impressed with eloquent speech or how sophisticatedly we can put words together in prayer, but with how real our hearts of compassion are toward Him. God is searching for pure hearts that desire to serve with no negative motives involved. When we have compassion to serve, we are laying down the very fundamental nature of who we are. Moreover, we hit a point of wanting to surrender ourselves, no matter the cost, because of who we are in Christ. Our consecrated spirits in us have to connect with who God is. Intricately, our spirits have to be knitted together with the will of the Father.

THE WATCHMAN (SEE EZEKIEL 3; 33)

We must always stay faithful to our church, no matter what, unless they are teaching contrary to the Word of God. We must be people of integrity and remain true to God and our leaders. The Bible says, *"Obey those who have rule over you"* (Heb. 13:7; 17 NKJV).

Continue to be the peacemaker when all else is crumbling and falling apart. In all that you do in work or deed, continue to fight against having a mindset of complaining or murmuring (see Phil. 2:14). Do not encourage it by listening to the mess that comes out of the mouths of other people. Walk in the Spirit and in the truth (see John 14:6). Travel with people you can trust. You cannot inform everyone of all your personal secrets, issues, desires, visions, and plans. Did you know that it takes anointing, ability, power, and authority to be able to handle your mess? This is true not only for a person's ability to hear your troubles, but also the ability to help you develop a blueprint in your mind for how to deal with your issues. There are people who are not able to handle it; it will do more damage than good—occasionally.

At other times, if you are not careful and you confess private information about yourself to people you thought you could trust, you may find yourself the subject of ridicule and gossip. This is a perfect example of the importance of discerning between your "associates" and those you call your "friends." Not everyone in your circle of influence will be compassionate about your personal matters; sharing with such people will only bring unnecessary contention and distress into your life.

Be in constant prayer and surround yourself with anointed people of God who can facilitate in the time of need and encourage you whenever you need aid. You need that life support to help you breathe when the enemy is seeking to strangle your dreams and choke your visions right out of your heart and spirit. Don't just rebuke when the enemy comes against you like a flood, but expel, destroy, repel, and resist him in the name of Jesus. And God will raise that standard for you and with you. He will stand triumphantly, and so will you in the name of the Lord Jesus!

Watch and pray always. As I said earlier, a "watchman" is considered a prophet in the Old Testament, but in other cases, such as these, it can mean to watch out for yourself and others in the spirit. Be wise as a serpent and yet gentle as a dove. Fight back in the spirit, and take back what the enemy has stolen from you; he has done enough after all these years of stealing, beating you down, and taking what never belonged to him in the first place.

I had to fight hard to get back what I had allowed the devil to take from me. Satan steals your visions, destroys your spirit, and devours your dreams—but only if you are unaware of the enemy's devices, tactics, and deceptions. You must understand that the enemy is very real and conniving, and he plays for keeps, with the goal of making sure your future is dark, cold, and unbearable. There are Christians who state that Jesus is their love, but they are wolves in sheep's clothing. And they will steal from you if you let them.

THE REALITIES OF HELL

Jesus knew that His image-bearers would not imagine the fact that a loving God could create such a horrific place of torment for anyone but the devil and his angels. I know that hell exists, not only because the holy men of God wrote about it in the Bible, but because I was actually allowed to come out of my body, experiencing the spirit realm firsthand. I would like to assure you hell is a real and tangible place in the center of the earth, as recorded in the Scriptures (see Matt. 12:40).

Let's look at the few Bible characters who were recorded as going to hell: Jonah, Jesus, and the rich man, (interestingly enough, several theologians and historians who would teach Wednesday night Bible study at my church found out the rich man's name, Mr. Divies), who all went to hell (two came back; one resided). After death, all the Old Testament prophets were in the center of the earth where hell was with only a chasm fixed between them. Antediluvians from ancient times, before Christ died, went to paradise adjacent exactly where hell is located. When Jesus died on the cross, He relocated paradise from the heart of the earth, and repositioned it into the third heaven, with a triumphal procession in the presence of His Father.

Here's what the Scriptures say about Jonah and Jesus:

*For as Jonas was three days and three nights in the **whale's belly**; so shall the Son of man be three days and three nights **in the heart of the earth** (Matthew 12:40).*

*Then Jonah prayed unto the Lord his God out of the fish's belly, and said, I cried by reason of mine affliction unto the Lord, and He heard me; **out of the belly of hell cried I**, and Thou heardest my voice (Jonah 2:1-2).*

*Then I said, I am cast out of Thy sight; yet I will look again toward Thy holy temple. The waters compassed me about, even to the soul: the depth closed me round about; the weeds were wrapped about my head. **I went down to the bottoms of the mountains**; the earth with **her bars** was about me forever: yet hast Thou brought up **my life from corruption**, O Lord my God. When my soul fainted within me, **I remembered the Lord; and my prayer went up unto Thee, into Thine holy temple** (Jonah 2:4-7).*

*Wherefore He saith, when He ascended up on high, **He led captivity captive**, and gave gifts unto men. Now that He ascended, what is it but that **He also descended first into the lower parts of the earth**? He that descended is the same also that ascended up far above all heavens, that He might fill all things (Ephesians 4:8-10).*

157

You will not find mountains or an earth with bars inside of a whale's stomach; Jonah died in the belly of the whale, which was symbolic, a parallel between Jesus and Jonah contrasting Jesus' death with Jonah's. No human can survive living in a stomach full of acid. (Stomach acid will severely burn skin. The pH level is 1-2, the same as hydrochloric acid.)

Jonah's soul started to descend, and as he was descending, he saw mountains, as well as the bars in hell, appearing in front of him. Jonah prayed and repented to God, and the Lord heard his plea, causing the whale to vomit him out onto dry land.

My point is, hell is an actual place with fire, fear, and undying hopelessness with no anticipation of ever getting out! Unfortunately, repentance does not exist for those who have died in their sins; hell becomes their eternal home. While we are yet alive, we can make the decision to accept Christ so we don't send ourselves to hell forever. We choose a path—either to die twice or to live twice. If we include physical death, it's really dying three times if we are in sin. According to Hebrews and Revelation (see Heb. 9:27; Rev. 2:11), sinners will die a natural death once and spiritual death twice. Born-again believers will live twice, unless they experience natural death on earth.

Let me explain: Sinners will die a natural death once on earth and then die a second time when placed in hades. Jesus said He is going to take hades and cast it into the lake of fire, which is considered hell—the third death (see Rev. 20:14). When the New Testament was written in the Greek, the English translators replaced the word *hades* with *hell*, when in true essence *gehenna* should be translated *hell* in the Gospels (see Matt. 10:28; Rev. 20:14). Revelation 14 is only speaking about spiritual death. Considering the possibility of a "second death," which path will we choose?

1. **The Sinners/Backsliders Path:** A sinner dies physically, *once*. Then the sinner dies a *second* time spiritually and is sent to hades/hell. Then the sinner dies a *third* time after the Great White Throne Judgment, which is a more horrible death then the second because the sinner is sent into the lake of fire to be tormented in the same place as the devil and his angels.

2. **Path of the Child of God:** Two paths are available to the child of God. On Path 1, the saint lives physically *once* (is raptured) and then lives again for all eternity (thus, the saint lives *twice*). On Path 2, the saint dies physically *once* (is not raptured) and then lives again for all eternity (thus, the saint dies once and then lives again).

According to tradition, hades or hell—whichever we feel most comfortable using—is considered to be like sweating in a very, very hot sauna. When the sinner is placed into the lake of fire, with the devil and his angels, that same sinner will be in the exact location suffering torment in agony and torture for all eternity because of rejecting Christ as Lord and Savior. This is one of the main reasons satan and his demons are trying very hard to get us back into sin and our old ways. His goal is to keep us where we are, making sure we don't get right with God; he wants our eternal future to be the same as his.

Regrettably, there are thousands of Christians who do not believe there is a devil or a literal hell. I believe if there was no hell then Jesus would have never revealed it in the Scriptures. Here are just a few of the passages in the Bible about hell:

> *If your hand causes you to sin, cut it off. It is better for you to enter into life maimed, rather than having two hands, to go to hell, into the fire that shall never be quenched. Where "Their worm does not die, and the fire is not quenched." And if your foot causes you to sin, cut it off. It is better for you to enter life lame, rather than having two feet, to be cast into hell, into the fire that shall never be quenched. Where "Their worm does not die, and the fire is not quenched." And if your eye causes you to sin, pluck it out. It is better for you to enter the kingdom of God with one eye, rather than having two eyes, to be cast into hell fire. Where "Their worm does not die, and the fire is not quenched"* (Mark 9:43-48 NKJV).

> *...The soul that sinneth, it shall die* (Ezekiel 18:4).

> *And as it is appointed for men to die once, but after this the judgment* (Hebrews 9:27 NKJV).

> *Is there not an appointed time to man upon earth? Are not his days also like the days of an hireling?* (Job 7:1)

And do not fear those who kill the body but cannot kill the soul. But rather fear Him [God] *who is able to destroy both soul and body in hell* (Matthew 10:28 NKJV).

THE GOD WHO SEES AND THE DEVIL WHO MIMICS

God's eyes run to and fro, looking for willing people whom He can utilize for His ministry to be able to develop and strengthen the Body of His Son. *"For the eyes of the Lord run to and fro throughout the whole earth, to show Himself strong in the behalf of them whose heart is perfect toward Him..."* (2 chron. 16:9). Further, He knows all that is in our hearts, and we will give account for it, whether good or bad, on the Day of Judgment. Jeremiah wrote, *"For My eyes are on all their ways; they are not hidden from My face, nor is their iniquity hidden from My eyes"* (Jer. 16:17 NKJV). Years later, the writer of Hebrews echoed this concept. *"And there is no creature hidden from His sight, but all things are naked and open to the eyes of Him to whom we must give account"* (Heb. 4:13 NKJV).

The devil has always attempted to copy, mimic, and imitate the Lord since the very beginning of his fall (see Isa. 14; Ezek. 28). In an instant, satan learned the hard way that he simply couldn't be greater than God. He is very well educated in the Scriptures, better than most Christians, and he impersonates the attributes of God—becoming as an angel of light throughout the course of history toward people.

In actuality, he is a hurricane of horrendous destruction and despair. Everything that satan touches spoils in his hands. He has no original ideas; his motto is, "Why not become the great copycat, since I cannot be the Most High God?" The Bible shows us what this kind of distorted thinking has done to him and the angels who followed after him, resulting in an everlasting stay in a world of eternal condemnation (see Ezek. 28:1-19)! According to First Peter 5:8, he goes to and fro in the regions of the earth seeking whom he may devour *"like a roaring lion." Like* in the text indicates a simile, a figure of speech, and an allegory. Therefore, he is *not* an actual lion, but he *acts* like one. He is an actor, and actor's act, but it's not the real story. He is a lion with no teeth, with a ramshackled mane. He is a defeated foe since Christ reigned as champion over him at the cross—the Lion of the Tribe of Judah triumphs over the one who is *like* a lion. Hallelujah!

> *Be sober; be vigilant; because your adversary the devil walks about like a roaring lion, seeking whom he may devour. Resist him, steadfast in the faith, knowing that the same sufferings are experienced by your brotherhood in the world* (1 Peter 5:8-9 NKJV).

KINGDOM-MINDED

Do not rely on yourself for a supernatural exchange if you are walking after the flesh; you will walk into a well of trouble that you don't want to encounter. Let the Holy Spirit breathe on you. Express your love to the Lord in your time of Holy Communion in prayer. This is the key element to knowing Him. The Almighty loves you more than you can ever love yourself! He loves your children more than you will ever love them.

We must learn to walk as conquerors. Conquerors know when they are conquered by love. Conquerors are kingdom-minded. There is a significant difference between a regular churchgoer and a conqueror—the vast difference between a child of God and to a son of God (I mentioned earlier that *son* is a mature term used of those who are walking in their inheritance now). Children of God have to wait until they are mature enough to be able to handle and walk in their inheritance. But conquerors in the spirit conquer in all areas of their lives, which is a character trait of "sons," who do not walk in defeat and vain words or lifestyles, but in obedience, prayer, and discernment. Various folks will come to us seeming to be harmless, but inside they are filled with conceit and dead men's bones. Conquerors will be able to discern the truth about these people and will have the wisdom to know how to deal with them.

The Lord desires for us to spend more time with Him. We must prepare for the coming of the Messiah. Part of the preparation is making sure our lives as a whole are in total submission to the will of God. Jesus said, *"Not my will, but yours be done"* (Matt. 26:39). Kingdom-mindedness always strives to rise above juncture and crisis. By no means do I speak or write about issues that I have not experienced myself. It's hypocritical to instruct others without making sure to do the same thing that I teach to others.

Be Kingdom-minded, think big, follow the vision that is set before you, take it and run with it without looking back. Move forward and bring destruction to the chasms of hell with every opportunity that comes your way. Win souls for the Glory of God the Father. In the name of Jesus, go and advance the King's dominion by force!

> *Yet in all these things we are more than conquerors through Him who loved us. For I am persuaded that neither death nor life, nor angels nor principalities nor powers, nor things present nor things to come, nor height nor depth, nor any other created thing, shall be able to separate us from the love of God, which is in Christ Jesus our Lord* (Romans 8:37-39 NKJV).

A *true Kingdom* frame of mind is to love God with all our existence—it will help us find our true character and uniqueness. In fact, He requires of us to love Him (see John 14:23). He knows the devil is doing all he can to pull us away from eternal life. We must not go down without a fight; the enemy has lost the battle and the war. Those who are not saved and are in sin, labeled as children of disobedience, I implore to think twice about the position they are in. After a while, the enemy will come to them and try to take over their minds, hearts, and eventually their spirits. Not having the Spirit of the Lord living in them will open a gateway for the devil to "come in and sup with them," just like Jesus mentioned in the Book of Revelation (see Rev. 3:20). Remember, satan is the great counterfeiter, the great impersonator. He causes many souls that are already lost to *hate* God and His people to prevent them from entering into the joys of oneness and partaking of Christ's Kingdom. The devil hates the children's *bread*—Jesus is that *bread*, which has come down from Heaven (see John 6:51). Keeping this in mind will make us wise to the devil's methods.

There is a warning in the Word that speaks about hating the Lord and not accepting who Jesus really is. *"But he who sins against Me wrongs his own soul; all those who hate me love death"* (Prov. 8:36 NKJV). Elsewhere it says, *"He who believes in Him is not condemned; but he who does not believe is condemned already, because he has not believed in the name of the only begotten Son of God"* (John 3:18 NKJV).

TRUTH REIGNS

Clearly, we know that preaching is proclamation and teaching is explanation. We need to teach more in our churches today. It's not enough to just preach what's already written; we need to go deeper with the Word of God. When people are being challenged with something devastating, they will need to be taught how to handle it; being inspired and motivated will not handle the situation. They need proper teaching and instruction to overcome their circumstances. I am not saying preaching doesn't have its proper place, but sometimes we need to get the right teaching to receive the right results. We must divide the Word of truth and teach the Bride of Christ lovingly and effectively (see 2 Tim. 2:15).

The apostle Paul was a teaching apostle, writing mostly to the Gentiles about the Messiah. He had such a heavy concern and burden for his people; we can hear it in his voice as he entreated them to walk on the road of salvation and redemption (see 2 Peter 3:15). In fact, Romans 6-9 is designated for the Jews. The Lord wanted Paul to address the Gentiles only after the Jews kept rejecting his message about the death of Christ on the cross. After all, the Jews kept trying to take Paul's life and forcing him into dreadful situations to stop him from preaching the light of life to all people.

Much can be learned from the apostles and the early church fathers, who worshiped God and trusted the Word completely and totally. That is the same attitude we must have as Christians *in the faith,* today. Belief always has a beginning; *faith* always is. As an acronym, we can read it: Fully Aware In Trusting Him.

Evidently, the Lord's will is to make certain that His everlasting Words of freedom become obvious in the lives of believers. This is certainly not the case with certain heresies that I've encountered in the last several years, causing bondage to run throughout the nation of America and abroad. I have witnessed and experienced many ministers within the Body of Christ taking passages out of context and using them to support their distorted views. Ministers in churches are teaching young people that there's nothing wrong with fornication, because it's not specifically forbidden in the Holy Bible. I believe in my heart (and I am sure you agree) that fornication is a sin. You shouldn't have sex with someone who is not your wife or husband (see 1 Cor. 6:13; 7:9). Consequently, the immorality of churchgoers and leaders has created wrong views that can really put new believers into confusion. This is especially tragic if they have a specific call on their lives, such as the offices of apostle or bishop.

Once, I had a pastor tell me that bishops are above apostles. What he failed to understand is that the *apostle* put those offices in place. They did not exist until the Great Apostle, Jesus, came onto the scene to create others like Himself and set those offices in proper placement. Not all are called to be apostles, prophets, teachers, evangelists, or pastors, but we must teach in detail what each office of the five-fold ministry actually does.

These issues are minuscule compared to the real troubles that exist in the four walls of the Church. You have to be mindful of the little foxes that destroy the vine (see Song of Sol. 2:15). The Lord doesn't base His prominence or thesis on how many degrees you have or how systematic your theology is. He is concerned more about the way you live your life in complete obedience to Him and His Word. The Bible has such little depth that a newborn believer can sip from it, yet is deep enough to drown the most celebrated theologian with all of his degrees. Don't get me wrong; I think theological seminary is wonderful. If that is where God is calling you, praise the Lord. Go for it in the name of Jesus—as long as neither you nor the professors try to minimize the character and mannerisms of God or how God manifests to His children, as others in some cases are doing.

The autonomy of God has complete capability to set up and break down kingdoms when He chooses to, with no permission from us. Putting God in a box like He is an action figure that we can pull out of our back pockets whenever they need to justify our sins is hazardous to our health—literally. It will only bring chaos and a fountain of perplexity. Focus and a good comprehension of spiritual themes will help us, in the long run, to maintain our composure and certainty in the Son of Man, even when the world throws us a curve ball of doubt.

It really grabs a hold of me when I see major subjects being taken so lightly, especially in the community and on television. Galatians 5:16-21 specifically lists all kinds of transgressions that will prevent anyone who travels down the path of self-pleasure and loose living from entering Heaven. One day my wife and I were watching a television program, and we came across a channel on which someone was advocating gay marriage and immoral behavior. I never say committing adultery is wrong. I never say that homosexuality is wrong. I say they are sins! When we confess that these immoral acts are *wrong*, the world knows how to go around the Word and make wrong right and legalize it, as if they had the power to do so.

In the end, the Lord will win, and sin will have its day. Sin is sin, regardless of how people try to deal with it or cover it up. When people cover their sins, they will not prosper in this life until they first, repent; second, confess to God; and third, ask for forgiveness and forsake the sin. Mercy will soon follow after. *"He who covers his sins will not prosper, but whoever confesses and forsakes them will have mercy"* (Prov. 28:13 NKJV).

GET UNDERSTANDING!

Multitudes choose not to walk in total freedom, but to walk in the periphery of holiness; they will never fulfill the mission God has for their lives and will never come to the richness of the indwelling of the Holy Spirit. The navigation and imprint of God's hand has already been impressed with the truth, but if the image-bearers don't get it straight and begin, instead, to refuse the call that is on their lives, they will be in a position of eternal discontentment. The Word declares plainly that such people are worthy of death! Our flesh must die and be in a state of total surrender to God when we are walking in His presence. There will be consequences if humility and walking in truth with His Spirit don't bring submission in our lives.

We will not be used of God if we become bound by a tradition that becomes greater than the Word of God. The writers of the Bible made it very clear, saying that all believers should cry out to God as "Abba" and seek out His understanding so that when the command is given it will fall on listening ears and obedient souls (see Rom. 8:15). If we admonish our leaders, who are guiding us into the arms of Christ, we will fall flat on our faces. Spiritually, individuals can destroy themselves very quickly. If Christians begin to wander away from the understanding that the Lord has set before them, He will give them warning after warning, placing caution signs in every area of their lives in order to cause them to repent and change their minds back to Him. When this happens, believers need to turn away from their disobedience immediately. Father God has mapped out the way clearly in His Son; all they have to do is walk into it and stay there with consistency and courage, without wavering. Here is what the Scripture says:

> *Without* ***understanding***, *covenant breakers, without natural affection, implacable, unmerciful: Who knowing the judgment of God, that* ***they which commit such things are worthy of death***, *not only do the same, but have pleasure in them that do them* (Romans 1:31-32).

> *The man that* ***wandereth out of the way of understanding*** *shall remain in the congregation of the dead* (Proverbs 21:16).

NO LIMITATIONS

What happens in the lives of Christians who really serve the Lord? The Spirit of God starts teaching us things that others will not understand. We have dreams that are unexplainable, yet so vivid with hidden messages they can make our toes curl. The message is clear and direct, and we get excited and find it difficult to wait and see what else God has planned for us. Then visions begin to occur when we are awake, showing us future events to get us moving forward in the Lord. These visions are sometimes so realistic it feels like we can grab and taste them. The moment we begin sharing these dreams and visions the Lord shared with us, like Joseph did with his brothers (see Gen. 37:5), people end up hating us or becoming jealous—even distant. There are the select few who will help us celebrate and assist us with shared enthusiasm—I call these people spiritual motivators.

As people of God, we must be cautious in every area of our lives, being very meticulous when we come into contact with spiritual parasites. When they begin to raise their ugly heads and try to drain us instantly—we must be discerning. Furthermore, no matter where we are in the world, we will have the spiritual ability of discerning spiritual parasites and spiritual hitchhikers. These people would like to take from us and pull from the giftings that God has placed deep down inside of us.

We have no idea what we are capable of until the Lord gets hold of us. Sometimes others will see us and something will rise up within them, like jealousy, envy, or the desire to decrease us. Only the Holy Spirit, who is truth and power, can help us with our walk, making sure that our vision is birthed and manifested into our reality. We must believe God and refuse to doubt His ability; He has the authority to bring it into fruition. When we start flowing in the anointing and the blessings begin to come to pass and are evident in our lives for many to see, we will see who is who (since the spirits of envy, jealousy, and covetousness are never far away). We must be very careful as image-bearers. We must know our true purpose and be aware of the enemy! These things happen so we can recognize the spirit of a Counterfeit Christian!

Many are not familiar with the Holy Spirit or where He actually dwells. He lives in the deepest part of a person. We must learn to hear the voice of the Lord, refusing to put limits on Him; He doesn't deserve to be lowered or limited. He already became low and limited Himself when He entered into the physical form of a man (see Heb. 10:5). We are not to do this any longer. People must stop telling God what to do and dictating to Him what His limits are. We need to hear Him a lot more clearly in these days.

When I was a child, I wondered where He actually lived.

IN MY BELLY?

The Spirit of the Lord lives right inside the deepest parts of our inner person, what we call our stomach area or our belly. In 1980, my family was living in the South Bronx; my mother and I were headed to my grandmother's house, and to my amazement, I saw half of a man walking on his hands and waist. I wondered how a person could live like that, and I asked myself "Gee, where does the Holy Spirit dwell?" I remembered the text where it says (my paraphrase) that the Spirit lives inside of our bellies. *"He that* *believeth on Me, as the scripture hath said, out of his **belly** shall flow rivers of living water"* (John 7:38). That was an awe moment for me, being ignorant to the fact that the living water is the Spirit of God. Our bellies are also known as our hearts, as in the New King James Version of this verse. In Proverbs it also says, *"The spirit of man is the candle of the Lord, searching all the **inward parts of the belly**"* (Prov. 20:27).

CAUTION!

At the age of 18, I met a man who was 28 years old who lived across the street from my mother's house. Knowing we had moved onto the block, he introduced himself to me saying he was a Muslim and that he had been inviting our neighbors to his mosque, notifying them about how inspirational his religion is. Eventually, the conversation became a dialogue about Jesus' Spirit. Refusing to believe that there is a Spirit of God who lives inside of people by invitation, he would always change the subject, repudiating that the Holy Spirit ever existed. As all Muslim's were known to do when I was growing up, they would constantly challenge the Lord's wisdom and knowledge from the passages of the Bible, arguing that Christians believe there are three separate gods. The following day, he said to me plainly, "There is no Holy Spirit as you say." I was really offended when he said that to me since I felt he was trying to discredit the Spirit of Christ and my faith—which he would do constantly. Truthfully, he had the upper hand since he was well educated in both the Qu'ran and the Bible; the plight of it all was the absolute fact that he knew God's written Word better than I did. The apostle Peter said it best, telling us to be prepared to give an answer for the hope we have in Jesus, but I wasn't prepared.

> But sanctify the Lord God in your hearts: and **be ready always to give an answer to every man** that asketh you a reason of the hope that is in you with meekness and fear (1 Peter 3:15).

Eventually, as the months went by, I ended up falling into this man's traps as he baited me with the hottest music, feeding my ego, claiming I was one of the best rap artists in the city. Becoming Muslim was the end result of this whole scheme he had going on. Desiring to fit in, having the overwhelming feeling of being an important part of something worthy, I was willing to let go of Jesus after all the good His Spirit had shown me.

I remember their version of being born again called the Sha'jada or Shah'ada. It was totally different then what I have read in books. No Spirit of God comes to live in you, but a dark spirit of deception and militancy. Don't get me wrong I am not trying to attack Islam, but only sharing my testimony. I have met some very respectful and peaceful Muslims in mosque and in my community who were very rigid and firm. Apparently, most are not violent or trouble-some in my experience, but as I began to study the Qu'ran and visit the mosque, things started to change all together. Although all Muslims are not terrorists, all terrorists that I see in the news are Muslim. Having that kind of infor-mation in my head didn't prevent me from walking with this person, who I will call Sean (not his real name). He would always make sure that I would not come into contact with the Spirit of God or fellowship with others in church.

Demure in his speech, he had a smooth way of building his conniving words to make it seem so innocent and coy; he would always fool me.

It was like his destiny and assignment were to make sure that I would not figure out what the devil was doing through him. Though I was living with my mother at the time, I would constantly be in his house for hours until dawn. Since he was a DJ, his house was the spot where all types of rap and R&B music would be played, with all his friends relaxing and hanging out talking about Islam and other dark and idle topics.

One day my best friend, Julio, came with me to Sean's house, and we stayed all night until 5 A.M. making music, laughing, and talking. Whew! We were tired. Well after that visit, Sean knew that Julio was a born-again Christian. Consequently, as we spent time at his house, occasionally Sean would bash Julio with his words for no apparent reason. This was going on for days, then weeks, then months. Every time Julio would go home early, Sean would badmouth him, His God, and Jesus. He believed that Jesus was a good man and a prophet, but at the same time talked bad about the Lord, always taking the Lord's name in vain. As I look back now, Sean and I walked in total confusion, being blind to the *devil's* scheme and deceptive conduct, which was causing my own downfall, though all of this was happening to me in plain view for me to see. Yet, I did nothing to stop it, knowing I was wrong and so was this religion.

DRIFTED

I started fading away further and further from the Church and other believers. I began to drift into Islam at full force without a care in the world about where I was headed. As time went on, part of me looked forward to visiting the mosque with Sean, and at the same time, noticed that my attitude was spinning out of control on a different level of distorted thinking. I started talking back to my mother and disrespecting my younger brothers constantly. Suddenly, a hatred for Caucasian people started rising up within me. Then the hatred was targeting everyone around me, and eventually I even started hating myself. I remember that people starting looking different to me; it was really creeping me out and scaring me.

Yet I kept going to mosque. In service, I met the Imam (teacher), one of the facilitators of the service and the teacher of the Qu'ran. The Imam spoke to me about the five books of Islam, saying I needed to purchase all five of those books. He reached over to a table behind him near the library by the counter and showed me a different book with a picture of a Caucasian doctor delivering a white baby with small horns and a pointed tail. The Imam said, "This is the reason why we call whites blue-eyed devils." Now keep in mind, this experience doesn't mean that all mosques are the same or that Imams are equal in their teachings; this was my own experience.

Four months had passed since I first started visiting those services, leaving the Lord, and passionately analyzing the Qu'ran had become my focus. I no longer had an interest for the Bible, and I pushed it to the side, getting ready to dump it. For some reason, something within me would not let me throw the Bible away in the garbage, yet I would not pick it up and read it. Attending mosque and reading the "Qu'ran" and the "Fur'qan al Haq" (one of the five books of Islam) was more important to me then attending church and reading a Bible from a white man's God and religion, compared to Allah. The knowledge that Islam means submission began to flood my mind with distorted views of how I saw Jesus and white people. When my mother would cook meat, I would make sure pork was not in any of my food because I thought the white man was trying to control and destroy my mind. This is one of the teachings of the Qu'ran.

One evening, while I was watching television in the living room, my mother entered and said, "Luis, I know lately you have been hanging out with Sean, and I don't like it. I overheard him talking to you about me. If you think for a second you are going to listen to him and try to tell me off when I correct you or even bad mouth me, you will have to move out of my house. I am your mother; you are to honor me!" I felt so small and embarrassed. I went to my room and didn't come out until the next day. While all of this was going on, Julio had no clue that in my heart he had become my enemy.

One night, as I was getting ready for bed, my room felt weird. I paid no mind and went to sleep and started to have these terrible dreams. Demons were visiting me in my sleep, giving me nightmares, and I remember the feeling of not being able to come out of my dream. Once I became aware of what was happening to me, I tried to come out of it, but I couldn't. Physically I was trying to yell out, Jesus! The demons would cover my mouth. (Notice that I didn't call out to Allah or Mohammed.) Finally, I came to myself, yelling out Jesus' name and those repulsive spirits left.

JESUS, IS THAT YOU?

A few nights later, after hanging out with Sean, I went home, prayed to Allah, and fell asleep. I had a second dream, and this dream felt so real and supernatural it amazes me even now, like it happened just yesterday. I really thought everything that happened in this dream was occurring for real; it was a very scaring feeling, worse then demonic spirits attacking me. In the dream, I saw myself in the morning getting out of bed. As I walked out of my house, on the right side of the cement porch to the front doorstep, I paused for a moment and looked around. It was a beautiful day. The street I lived on looked exactly as it did in real life.

Unexpectedly, a loud noise thundered in the first heaven—the sky. I saw from the corner of my eye an image. I made a complete turn to have a better look and saw, at about the height where a plane would fly, a huge man in all white was walking toward Julio's house. Angels, who were a little shorter than the man, were bouncing behind Him, leaping for joy, walking, and passing me by like I didn't exist. Immediately what came into my mind was, *Whoa! This is Jesus! This is the rapture, this is the end!* I started to run eastward down my street, yelling in a loud voice, "Jesus! Jesus! Don't forget me!" He simply ignored me like I wasn't even there.

This dream felt so real it was phenomenal; it really felt like it was literally happening. I kept waving my hands and running with all that was in me toward Him, saying, "Jesus, don't forget me. It's me, Luis! It's me! It's me!" He kept on walking, and the angels paid me no mind. My cries fell on deaf ears. An unexplainable fear began to overtake me. This fear was Holy! When the fear of the Lord falls on you, it pushes you down to your knees, especially when you are not right with God. This fear was causing my knees to buckle, and I became very weak. Thereafter, I was violently pushed out of my dream with tremendous force, and my heart started racing really fast.

That morning when I awoke, before my mind could catch up to the fact that I was up (if that makes sense), I heard the Lord's voice say, "Go!" I knew exactly what that meant. I made haste and got dressed, running straight to Julio's house, covering about two blocks in less than five minutes. I knocked at his door like a madman, completely out of breath, until Julio opened the front door. I did not know he knew about all the garbage Sean and I were saying about him. I said to him, "Julio, I'm so sorry for what I have done to you. I didn't mean to talk bad and start false rumors about you. I don't know what came over me. Can you still be my friend? Do you forgive me? I am so sorry."

He replied, "I forgave you when I first heard you were talking bad about me." When he said that, I broke out into tears. The love of Christ was deep in his heart; it cut me like a knife through my soul and spirit. I had expected him to hate me and to give me in return what I had given him, but he proved me wrong, and we hugged. Ever since the dream and our reconciliation that day at Julio's parents' house, the spirits that were holding me down broke off of me. When God spoke to me, it shattered the strong man that was controlling me immediately. The chains of spiritual blindness and the bondage of tortuous lies exploded into flames in the spirit, instantly!

In all the months of serving Allah, not once had I read anything about him loving his children or dying for me; you will not find it in any of the surahs, or chapters, in the Qu'ran. He is not to be considered as a Father or as having children either; there is no love that I have found throughout the entire surahs of the Qu'ran. Not once, when I had a very critical need or was experiencing hard problems, did Allah speak to me and let me know everything was going to be OK. The devil is a liar!

I never did go back to Sean's house again. As I said before, every wolf has paws, so check their feet; the devil is under it, so check their feet; it is not beautiful nor does it bring good news. As it says in the Bible, *"The **steps** of a good man are ordered by the Lord, and He delights in his way"* (Ps. 37:23 NKJV) and *"...How beautiful are the **feet** of those who preach the gospel of peace, who bring glad tidings of good things"* (Rom. 10:15 NKJV).

I was made totally free! Although Sean looked for me, I made sure my availability to him was lost. Eventually that friendship starved and died. I spoke death to that terrible relationship; it really needed to die and stay dead. Like I always hear others and myself say, the anointing breaks the yoke of bondage (see Isa. 10:27). We all must learn from each other. We need each other on a daily basis. Wolves and counterfeit Christians come in like manner—kind, gentle, and understanding at first, but their agenda is to kill you!

WAKE UP!

It makes no difference where you are in the world reading this book; as long as you have a voice and a body with breath, it is never too late to get it right with Jesus. Do not condemn yourself by your own standards; the sin might be terrible and may be very great, but when God sees His Son's blood, which was shed on the cross, it is much greater than you could ever imagine. When people say that Jesus and His shed blood on Calvary were a stupid idea or they reject that kind of love, in reality, it's like smacking God in

His face. It's like telling the Lord, scoffing, "Hmph! Is this what you sent to earth to die for me, a man named Jesus? He is not worth it." When unbelievers turn against the Lord, they are *demon*strating that the gift God gave—His own Son to die in our place—is something hollow, obscure, and not good enough, a waste of time.

Wake up, people! The time of the end is upon us; we must worship God in His Spirit and in His truth. Jesus' death on the cross is none of these wicked things, but the power of God, manifested for all to see and accept with a contrite and broken spirit of surrender to His will.

Do not harden your hearts from the one who paid such a high price.

> *Therefore, as the Holy Spirit says: "Today, if you will hear His voice, do not harden your hearts as in the rebellion, in the day of trial in the wilderness"* (Hebrews 3:7-8 NKJV).

The Holy Spirit is waiting on you, Sister.

The Holy Spirit is waiting on you, Brother.

God has His arms wide open to receive you totally and completely. Torn down and broken on the inside or on the outside, it makes no difference with the Lord. Let him who stole, steal no more, I say, let him who gossiped, gossip no more (see Eph. 4:28). The Almighty Savior is waiting for you.

If you are already saved, I ask you these questions; answer truthfully:

- Can people tell you are saved?

- Can others see that milk and honey reside in the atmosphere of your heart?

- Do they feel the land of promise overcoming them with your humility and overflowing meekness?

- Do they feel offended or distant from you every time you leave their presence?

If you have some negative dealings weighing you down in your mind and your spirit, I encourage you right now to put your thoughts down on paper. Pray over them, as you represent it to God. It would be a good time to do that right now. This will be your time to meditate over those issues and give them to God; the burden is too much for you to carry. Men, I exhort you to take a moment and reflect truly on what you might need to write down to help you pray against what might be holding you back from confessing to God and forsaking whatever it is you are dealing with. I always see women reflect, but rarely see the men do it. I implore anyone reading this book to write *it* down and make it plain for you and God to see. Let's do it! In Jesus' name, let's bind that thing and loose His freedom and promises into our lives like a cascade.

And I will give you the keys of the kingdom of heaven, and whatever you bind on earth will be bound in heaven, and whatever you loose on earth will be loosed in heaven (Matthew 16:19 NKJV).

Write the vision and make it plain on tablets, that he may run who reads it. For the vision is yet for an appointed time, but at the end it will speak, and it will not lie. Though it tarries, wait

for it, because it will surely come, it will not tarry
(Habakkuk 2:2-3 NKJV).

HEARTFELT MEDITATIONS

*This Book of the Law shall not depart from your
mouth, but you shall **meditate** in it day and night,
that you may observe to do according to all that is
written in it. For then you will make your way
prosperous, and then you will have good success*
(Joshua 1:8 NKJV).

*Let the words of my mouth and the **meditation** of
my heart be acceptable in Your sight, O Lord, my
strength and my Redeemer* (Psalm 19:14 NKJV).

Have you forgotten the old saying, "Sinners run from
God, and saints run to God?" You always must be in a
mindset of total surrender, walking in His faith (see Heb.
11:6). In order to accomplish freedom and truth, you must
stay away from the attributes and characteristics that can
cause you to become a carnal and counterfeit Christian,
especially if you have no intention to change for the better.
Nevertheless, hold your ground and war against the negative and demonically inspired elements set before you by
your adversary.

- Adultery

- Accusation

- Apathy

- Backbiting

- Backsliding

- Bitterness

- Complacency

- Contention

- Debauchery

- False humility

- Fantasy lust

- Fits of rage

- Gossip

- Gluttony

- Greed

- Hate

- Haughty spirit

- Idolatry

- Loose living

- Lukewarmness

- Lust

- Lying

- Pride

- Rebellion

- Sexual immorality

- Strife

- Theft

- Uncontrolled anger

- Unforgiveness

- Witchcraft

And the list goes on and on. Heed *red flags!* Stay away from exercising the items on this list as best you can. If you are struggling with something listed above, I encourage you to pray to the Lord and be totally real with Him. If you need help, call someone you can trust, who is a strong believer in the Lord. There is nothing worse than someone who walks in the office of hypocrisy and artificiality. The Bible says, *"Confess your trespasses to one another, and pray for one another, that you may be healed. The effective, fervent prayer of a righteous man avails much"* (James 5:16 NKJV).

Let's all bow our heads to a God who desires to be worshiped and praised. Let's make it our goal to live life day by day in the authority and virtue of the Holy Spirit, allowing the fruit of the Spirit to resonate in our members, being vigorous for the Kingdom always, and worshiping Him in Spirit and in Truth.

PRAYER

Lord, I come before you in humility. Praying that change will take over me as I continue to obey You so Your will can be done in my life. I may not have the understanding to discern all that needs to be discerned, but I have faith to believe that

You are going to help me in these areas. Lord God, put people in my life who are good for me that can teach me all things regarding You. If there are influences, even certain people in my life that are no good for me that I am not aware of, I pray now that You will remove them lovingly, to bring forth individuals who are healthy for me spiritually. Trusting You is my access to truth. Trusting you is not always meant for me to lean on my own understanding, but acknowledging You always when the time of leaning makes no sense to me. In this way, my paths can be straightened. Jesus, You are the Way, the Truth, and the Life. Bring this truth to my memory when satan and others attempt to discourage me in my everyday walk with You. Encourage me to rely on You always. Reveal to me what I need from You, in order to make sure Your will is done for my life. Blessed Savior, I also pray that You continuously bless and show mercy to my family. We need you more than ever in these last days. I will set these words upon my heart; I am more than a conqueror because of what You've accomplished at the cross. Thank you Jesus for saving my soul as well as my family. In Jesus' name, Amen!...

CHAPTER SEVEN

Knock. Knock. Who Is It? L.U.S.T.

I say then: walk in the Spirit, and you shall not fulfill the lust of the flesh. For the flesh lusts against the Spirit, and the Spirit against the flesh, and these are contrary to one another, so that you do not do the things that you wish.

—GALATIANS 5:16-17 NKJV

For the grace of God that brings salvation has appeared to all men, teaching us that, denying ungodliness and worldly lusts, we should live soberly, righteously, and godly in the present age.

—TITUS 2:11-12 NKJV

As we keep living life and grow older, we are encircled with diverse kinds of temptations. Believers have to be prepared and equipped when *lust* and *fantasy lust* come their way. *Lust* is defined in two different ways:

1. Strong sexual and sensual desire toward another person

2. Intense longing for something (like power or control)

My acronym for lust is:

Lust

Unifies

Sex and

Temptations

LUST UNIFIES SEX AND TEMPTATIONS

As we study the sacred Word of the Lord, we will notice that, from Genesis to Revelation, lust is not merely sexual. Lust is also linked to people's evil desires and greed related to materialism and self-gratification. As James wrote:

> *But every man is tempted, when he is drawn away of his own lust, and enticed. Then when lust hath conceived, it bringeth forth sin: and sin, when it is finished, bringeth forth death* (James 1:14-15).

Scripture tells us that we must come against and cast down these kinds of thoughts and actions in our everyday living (see 2 Cor. 10:5).

The association of *lust* with sexual behaviors has been amplified in the Church and the world. Lust is not only slipping its ways of perversion into the house of the Lord, but also into society everywhere. Pornography is destroying lives, homes, and marriages, which are falling apart every minute. Recently, I heard a pastor state that the divorce rate among Christians is surpassing the divorce rate of the world's matrimonies. Centuries ago, Paul described this:

> *You must understand this: In the last days there will be violent periods of time. People will be selfish and love money. They will brag, be arrogant, and use abusive language. They will curse their parents, show no gratitude, have no respect for what is holy, and lack normal affection for their families. They will refuse to make peace with anyone. They will be slanderous, lack self-control, be brutal, and have no love for what is good. They will be traitors. They will be reckless and conceited. They will love pleasure rather than God. They will appear to have a godly life, but they will not let its power change them. Stay away from such people* (2 Timothy 3:1-5 GW).

Now this spirit is overflowing into our young people, the saved and the unsaved, the churchgoer and the non-churchgoer. They all are arriving in a harmful arena, knowing they will never return from their fornications and wicked deeds—*chiefly* because their consciences are seared. Paul said of them, *"...Their minds are corrupt, and the faith they teach is counterfeit"* (2 Tim. 3:8 GW).

The Lord God has designed since the beginning of time for us to stay away from *all* kinds of sensual, sexual, and lustful sins. Lust is one of the deadliest aspects of our sinful nature, alongside debauchery. When lust and debauchery are united, they contain the power to open us up to various fiend spirits, imps, demons, the spirit of Delilah, pornography, the spirit of Potiphar's wife, and Belial. These spirits have the power spiritually and physically to overpower us, causing mental slavery. Only the Holy Spirit and the anointing can break the despotism over our lives! Those who have been overcome by any of these malicious spirits—and they do work as a team—will need a man or woman of God anointed with a powerful deliverance ministry to assist in breaking the cycles of generational curses and familiar spirits that such people may have invited into their inner circle. Deliverance is needed in order to be made free from these types of strongholds; this is very vital in the lives of believers.

This enticement of wantonness is very powerful. Like a drug, it takes people into a world of false hopes and dreams. Society as a whole is collapsing right in front of us because of this, and we have no idea how to stop it. But we serve a God who holds everything in the power of His Name. Here is Heaven's strategy:

- First, war against it with the spirit of prayer.

- Second, defeat the enemy by not taking part in his false endeavors.

- Third, fast for what is good and abstain from evil desires of all sorts.

The lifestyle of promiscuity and distorted views of sex are running this great country of ours down to total destruction—in the natural as well as in the spiritual. Corrupt mentalities, combined with strong lustful envy, have created an impish culture consumed with pornography, which has evolved into a multi-billion dollar a year industry, surpassing alcohol and drugs combined. Lechery is a powerful weapon that we have pursued in our flesh and our souls without giving ear to the many consequences, which are very significant. As the years have gone by, the Church has stopped speaking about these issues because of the explicit nature and graphic content of it. However, it is so critical in the days we are living in (see Hos. 4:6). Saints have to be transformed mentally according to the well-timed Scriptures the apostle Paul wrote about in Romans:

> *I beseech you therefore, brethren, by the mercies of God, that you **present your bodies** a living sacrifice, **holy**, acceptable to God, which is your reasonable service. And **do not be conformed to this world**, but be **transformed by the renewing of your mind**, that you may prove what is that good and acceptable and perfect will of God (Romans 12:1-2 NKJV).*

SPIRITUAL SUICIDE

Demons do not force us to fall into the hands of a Jezebel spirit; we invite it in by a willing heart. Sometimes believers will say things like, "The devil made me do it," or "I couldn't help it, the temptation was just too strong to fight off." There's a fine line between an excuse and a person who is willing to sin. Reality is, such people have been entertaining the images and thoughts that entered the theatres of their minds without taking into consideration that they are suppose to cast those iniquitous mental movies down:

> **Casting down imaginations**, and every high thing that exalteth itself against the knowledge of God, and bringing into captivity every thought to the obedience of Christ; and having in a readiness to revenge all disobedience, when your obedience is fulfilled (2 Corinthians 10:5-6).

If an image comes into our minds, we have less than three seconds to cast it down before it gets to our hearts. Once it gets into our souls—our hearts—it is too late. We are already ensnared by the wicked deceitfulness of your own desires. As the prophet Jeremiah wrote, *"The **heart is deceitful** above all things, and **desperately wicked**: who can know it?"* (Jer. 17:9).

LUST OF THE FLESH

Nowhere in Scripture do we find a demonic spirit of lust explicitly named, though many passages mention lust. Romans 6:12 says, *"Let not sin therefore reign in your mortal body, that ye should obey it in the lusts thereof."* And in James 1:14, it says, *"But every man is tempted when he is drawn away of his own lust, and enticed."* *Enticed* means to: attract with pleasure and reward. Written by the apostles to caution the Body of Christ, the purpose of these verses was to instruct us how to prevent sin from reigning in our mortal bodies and, therefore, prevent us from obeying lust. John said of lust: *"For all that is in the world the lust of the flesh, lust of the eyes, and the pride of life, is not of the Father, but is of the world"* (1 John 2:16).

Fifty Scriptures discuss lust but never state that it is a demonic spirit. It's our *own* lust that we must bring into subjection to God's Holy Word—every day. We fight it with Scripture, consecration, quotes of warfare, prayer, and fasting—these are the keys to overcoming this entire ordeal. Lust opens doors to the evil spirit named *Belial;* all kinds of perverted spirits are under his authority. He sends them to tempt us, but no spirits come into us to force us to fall into sin—unless they are willingly invited.

Distorted sexual views and openness will unlock spiritual portals that will be hard to close. Evil spirits will physically and spiritually destroy us and keep us longer than we ever intended. When they are done with us, we will be dead! We must fall on our faces in the sight of God in these evil days, as it gets darker and darker by the minute. So many movies and television shows contain vulgar words that were never allowed when I was a child; now they are televised with no conscience or ethics. Sex and vulgarity are being amplified and exhibited graphically; we must work harder than ever to filter these things so our children don't have to hear and see the perversion of the world's social disorder.

The Lord has made a way for Christians to take the Word of God and run with zeal for the Good News of Christ in order to protect the moral values that we have left. We must take holiness and purity by force immediately, or we will stumble before the King of kings! As living sacrifices, we have to deny ourselves when it comes to our evil desires and wants. The Spirit of the Lord will help and guide us *if* we call on His Name. We are living in a desperate and chaotic age, but God has a plan to redeem and refresh us all in the near future. Hanging on to what is good is the duty of all those who are saved and Holy Ghost-filled. We must endure until the end and fight with wisdom so that we may experience the refreshing that is coming. We must be ready always and fight our flesh until the end, and we will be rewarded.

> *Therefore let him who thinks he stands take heed lest he fall. No temptation has overtaken you except such as is common to man; but God is faithful, who will not allow you to be tempted beyond what you are able, but with the temptation will also make the way of escape, that you may be able to bear it* (1 Corinthians 10:12-13 NKJV).

Authentic Christians must want the relief only Christ can give in order to walk in liberty. The Holy Spirit will see we are serious. If we hold true, He will start to burn in us like a fire within our members—captivating our minds and souls with piety, making us complete and whole on the inside. He will cause us to put a halt on our cravings that are contradictory to God's laws and His mental map of holiness so that we can walk in His freedom.

KNOCK. KNOCK. WHO IS IT? LUST!

Worship Warriors
Spiritual Successors
Power Praisers
Obedient Servants

This is who we are in the Lord. It's Christ who rewards us openly, operating in and satisfying the empty and the fallen. Feeling like a failure, yet we are successful; having conflict and disruption on all sides, yet we have a battle cry on reserve. Let's adjust ourselves and be prepared. Lust will constantly knock on the doors of our hearts, but when it does knock, we have to let it knock and never answer. (No matter how many times we say *no,* it will still knock on occasion because we are still incased in flesh.)

Singles who are sexually frustrated must go above and beyond what is expected. Jesus will always be there to give you the strength that you need, enabling you to do all things through Him (see Phil. 4:8; 9,13). Depend on God with all of your might! The Words says to, *"Be strong in the Lord and in the power of His might"* (Eph. 6:10). God promises that you don't have to do it in your own power.*"…Not by might, nor by power, but by My Spirit says the Lord of hosts"* (Zech. 4:6). He has provided your way of escape.

The Lord will be Lord forever—that is His name! He is the King who will reign eternally, and His decrees and mannerisms are from everlasting to everlasting. *Ad infinitum* belongs to our God. After dissecting the plans of the enemy in order to know our true purpose in our lives, the gift of infinity will not be given to us if we fall into the company of evil desires and camp there. The angels called Goodness and Mercy are our stepping-stones, following us throughout our years, like they once did for David of the Old Testament (see Ps. 23:6).

Some time ago I tried to amend myself with my own authority, trying to set myself free, not knowing that freedom from bondage comes only through the influence of Jesus' Spirit. The Bible says, *"Many are the afflictions of the righteous, but the Lord delivers him out of them all"* (Ps. 34:19 NKJV). Now I know to take comfort in His existence, which is above all. Righteous people who encounter concupiscence, or strong sexual desire, must learn to deflect lust through the influence of God's Spirit of purity, who resists depraved ambitions, whether sexual or not. We must surround ourselves with the presence of the Lord above; a salacious spirit will be subject to the Spirit of Christ, who can never co-exist with evil when sitting on the right side of the throne of power in our hearts! All born again believers who have their names written in the Lamb's Book of Life are seated in heavenly places (see Eph. 2:6-7). Glory to God! No matter what we face, God promises us: *"Therefore submit to God. **Resist** the devil and he will flee from you. Draw near to God and He will draw near to you..."* (James 4:7-8 NKJV).

A KING WITH A SECRET

Lust was a downfall for one of the greatest Kings who ever walked the face of the earth, King David, the prophet of the Great God Yahweh. From his palace, King David watched Bathsheeba, another man's wife, as she was taking a *bath*. Not only did he watch, but he gave into his yearning for Bathsheeba, eventually making her pregnant. Afterward, he contemplated within himself how he would kill

Bathsheeba's husband, Uriah the Hittite, so that he could have her. Using his power wrongly fed the dark abyss of his own lust, and he misused his authority to deceive in order to get what he wickedly desired. When he did receive what he craved, it was more than he could bear (see 2 Sam. 11-12). David learned his lesson; it was a very difficult trail for him to walk on.

LUST FOR REPUTATION AND RICHES

The story of Samson and Delilah is an account in the Bible of betrayal between two consenting adults who were engulfed with unequal passion for each other for the wrong reasons. Samson lusted after Delilah because of her beauty, and Delilah lusted after Samson because greed for 1,100 pieces of silver (which were offered as a reward for Samson's capture) took over her.

> *Afterward it happened that he loved a woman in the Valley of Sorek, whose name was Delilah. And the lords of the Philistines came up to her and said to her, "Entice him, and find out where his great strength lies, and by what means we may over-power him, that we may bind him to afflict him; and every one of us will give you eleven hundred pieces of silver. (Judges 16:4-5).*

Needless to say, the Bible points out countless others who fell in a similar snare because of greed, lust, and a desire for control. Nonetheless, God has proven Himself faithful to all of His servants by modifying their lives into something great. God ultimately used Samson to destroy many Philistines (Israel's enemy), even while he was in bondage. God loves to knock the devil off of his platform of pride and prevent him from driving the people of God into nothingness.

SATAN, THE GREAT COUNTERFEITER

As we know, satan is the great counterfeiter; he will mimic his way into every tiny crack available to him, with the goal of making sure we follow hard after him, giving our lives to pride and false worship. We must be very discerning and aware of his wicked ideas and false wonders. These terrible times are beginning to manifest his children in places and positions that we never thought possible. Pastors are turning into witches; bishops are turning into warlocks; false teaching is everywhere; false signs are far and wide. Ultimately, they are *all* counterfeits of evil and spirits of malice! Treacherous behavior will emerge, as a result, causing iniquity to enter into the hearts of multitudes around the planet. It's about to get darker, but at the same time, *God* will manifest His power through His Light on earth—the Church!

THE WORD IS NEVER DONE

In the Old Testament writings of the prophets, we read of all the troubles they had to face, but they still held on to what was good for the Will of God (see Exod. 4; 1 Kings 19). When we compare recorded events of the past with real life events of today, we see that there are equivalent issues that have been going on since the very beginning of time. The egotistic concepts and ideas in our times mirror deceptions from ages past. Solomon wrote that there is nothing new under the sun, and it is still true (see Eccl. 1:9). Placing ourselves in "the Hands of Victory" will be challenging at first; yet the reward will be far greater as He continues to mold us into His likeness. After He takes us out of the fire and we are looking beautiful, even then He is not done with us. The work always continues until our change comes. God's ways are so divergent. He desires for us to be transformed by the renewing of our minds so that we will stay that way (see Rom. 12:1-2). Transformation is necessary to help us thwart the traps of satan and the lusts of our flesh and the world.

Those who say that God is understanding of our wallowing in sin, that He will not allow judgment to be executed on our lives, are only self-deceived. Here is a warning that the apostle Paul wrote to the people of Galatia. *"Walk in the spirit and you will not fulfill the lust of the flesh"* (Gal. 5:16). From Genesis to Revelation, we read about "the lust of the flesh" (not "the spirit of lust") and the damage it has caused all through history. Christ and the apostles understood this. The apostle Paul expressed it in Romans 7:14-21, detailing his personal struggles while being single.

CALL NO MAN FATHER?

Lust, whether spiritual, soulish, or natural, is sin in the eyes of Christ. Consider this carefully: When Jesus said, *"Call no man father"* (Matt. 23:9), He was not telling us to not call our natural dads, *father;* rather, I believe He foreknew that Catholicism would arise after He ascended to His heavenly Father and He was addressing an error in that belief. In Catholicism, a priest (who is called "father") goes into one side of a booth, and lay Catholics enter the opposite side of the same booth. A dialogue ensues between them, resulting in private confessions of all types, including sinful activities that the lay person has committed. These confessions always culminate with the request of the priest, "Father, forgive me for I have sinned."

After years and years of known and unknown members confessing their sins to the priest, a transformation begins to take place in the soul and spirit of the priest, most times unknowingly. Opening the ear gate of the soul for years, listening to admissions of sin and vulgar behavior can quickly destroy a life in many ways. Jesus plainly said (I'm paraphrasing), "Don't confess your sins to mere people because they are just that—people. They don't have the authority or the supremacy to forgive us, nor are they able to wash our sins away and repel the weight of sin" (see Mark 2:7). If we ponder what Jesus said, we will see that it makes total and complete sense. Confessing all kinds of sins, lies, lust issues, and everything under the sun will put a priest to his knees, opening portals to satanic oppression (keep in mind that most Catholic priests are not born-again Christians).

Here is the result of this religious process; we see them on the news for molestation, rape, or sodomy charges— sometimes all of the above. It's rare to see a pastor or a prophet on the news for such crimes. I am sure somewhere in our country and in our world it's happening; we are not to be naïve of that fact, but it's not as frequent or as televised. If a pastor or anyone in ministry is guilty of the same behavior in the presence of Christ, it will not go unpunished, even if it's not televised or in the morning paper.

We have the Holy Spirit to convict us and guide us. God allows us to be married, in part so that our minds do not travel farther than our flesh should go. Sadly, too often the Catholic priests are either expelled or excluded from the Vatican or the Catholic Church. When we realize the filth a Catholic father goes through, listening to the heaviness of sin, it becomes clear that priests do not have the capability to maintain a pure heart and mind before God in this environment. The heart is so deceitfully wicked how can anyone understand or know it (see Jer. 17:9). This is true because sin is a great burden to carry. The end result is that people (in this instance, priests) act out what has been poured into them. Countless priests have kept themselves from women, yet have different people from all walks of life visiting and confessing month after month and year after year their sexual immoralities. Eventually it will take a hold on them sexually. The sins of men are too heavy for a mere people to deal with.

God has created us to be sexual beings, but in the confines of marriage and not in fornication and promiscuity. Lust is very powerful, especially when we feed it. Not everyone will act on every thought or devious behavior that enters their minds, but many will eventually act on some of those thoughts. We all must be clever to know the designs of the devil and how he is trying to destroy us. We must be aware of the enemy and know our true purpose. The apostle Paul addressed this in First Corinthians 7:9, "...*If they cannot exercise self-control, let them marry. For it is better to marry than to burn with passion*" (NKJV), as well as in Ephesians 4:

> *This I say, therefore, and testify in the Lord, that you should no longer walk as the rest of the Gentiles walk, in the futility of their mind, having their*

understanding darkened, being alienated from the life of God, because of the ignorance that is in them, because of the blindness of their heart; who, being past feeling, have given themselves over to lewdness, to work all uncleanness with greediness. But you have not so learned Christ, if indeed you have heard Him and have been taught by Him, as the truth is in Jesus: that you put off, concerning your former conduct, the old man which grows corrupt according to the deceitful lusts, and be renewed in the spirit of your mind, and that you put on the new man which was created according to God, in true righteousness and holiness (Ephesians 4:17-24 NKJV).

LUST FOR POSITION AND POWER

Considering Peter to be the first Pope (which is a prominent Catholic teaching) has confused millions of people, knowing that Popes have no dealings with women or marriage. Yet Peter had a mother-in-law, and the only way he could have a mother-in-law was if he was married to the daughter (see Luke 4:38). This shows how people take the Scriptures out of context and distort the true character and nature out of the Word, misconstruing what the Lord was trying to relay to humankind. Misinterpretation can be a very powerful arsenal, if we are not careful. This coincides in the same characteristics of Christianity and the Bible. We must make sure how we live and everything we teach is according to the Word of God for purity and righteousness.

We often misinterpret the signs of sexual promiscuity and perversion. We have to be wise beyond our years, read our Bibles, and spend lots of time with God in prayer. Think of prayer as "powerful resources at our earliest request":

> Be anxious for nothing, but in everything by prayer and supplication, with thanksgiving, **let your requests be made known to God**; and the peace of God, which surpasses all understanding, will guard your hearts and minds through Christ Jesus (Philippians 4:6-7 NKJV).

SATAN, SIN, AND SEDUCTION

The one thing I can say with certainty is that there is victory if we are obedient and willing to follow hard after God, despite the problems stirring in the very apex of your intelligence. Many of us know better, yet we keep dabbling in sin and its nature. This should not be so. We must consecrate ourselves and give our all to the Lord Jesus Christ, without turning back, like the wife of Lot, when she turned into a pillar of salt (see Gen. 19:26). She looked back, which was a metaphoric sign of the attitude, "I don't want to start afresh; I miss my old life." This attitude violates this principle from Luke: *"Jesus said to him, 'No one, having put his hand to the plow, and looking back, is fit for the kingdom of God'* (Luke 9:62 NKJV). The leading of the Spirit of Christ will enable us to make it. Let's tell our friends—a sister, a brother, saved or unsaved—that they can make it as long as they have the Spirit of Life within them.

Satan is a liar and the father of lies (see John 8:44). Whether we lust after material things, control, authority, power, or sexual pleasures, unless we deal with it quickly, we will be shaken and shattered. Believers must adhere to the Word and the Lord's commandments and stay away from satan's craftiness; he is constantly releasing snares to captivate us with impious seductions. I have seen worldly people right along with Christians fall on their faces quickly because of lust; at other times, it happens slowly. But the devil will make sure it happens, guaranteed! Evil spirits know who we are and whether we are really serving the Lord or just being counterfeit. They are very daring and will expose us, if we prove to be false, to those around us.

Look at this account from the early Church:

> *Now God worked unusual miracles by the hands of Paul, so that even handkerchiefs or aprons were brought from his body to the sick, and the diseases left them and the evil spirits went out of them. Then some of the itinerant Jewish exorcists took it upon themselves to call the name of the Lord Jesus over those who had evil spirits, saying, "We exorcise you by the Jesus whom Paul preaches." Also there were seven sons of Sceva, a Jewish chief priest, who did so. And the evil spirit answered and said, "Jesus I know, and Paul I know; but who are you?" Then the man in whom the evil spirit was leaped on them, overpowered them, and prevailed against them, so that they fled out of that house naked and wounded* (Acts 19:11-16 NKJV).

In years of ministry, I have witnessed first hand what it means when someone tries to *mock* the ways of God. Thinking that they alone have the power to rebuke devils without knowing who Jesus is. The passage above proves beyond any reason that if you are not in an intimate relationship with the Lord, devils will not recognize who you are, therefore having access to hurt you in the process.

If we don't take this seriously, demons will have a field day in our thought lives. They will bombard us with all kinds of miscellaneous temptations; graphic images will be displayed in our minds to knock us off track. The Bible says, *"Now the Lord is the Spirit; and where the Spirit of the Lord is, there is liberty"* (2 Cor. 3:17 NKJV). Let's commit to memory the promises that when the Son makes us free, we are free indeed (see John 8:36) and that liberty in Christ breaks the yoke of bondage (see Gal. 5:1).

There is a big difference between being *set free* and *made free*. Allow me to paint a picture of the differences between the two. Being *set free* is when inmates, who are locked up in jail cells, are released; yet they are still behind bars of pure bondage in their hearts, minds, and spirits, even while their bodies are experiencing freedom. Being *made free* is when people receive Christ as Lord and Savior; they will experience liberty whether locked behind bars or not because the anointing destroys the yoke of mental and spiritual slavery. This allows anyone to experience genuine freedom with joy. *"Therefore if the Son **makes you free**, you shall be free indeed"* (John 8:36 NKJV). This is the true liberation of Christ. So let's walk audaciously and not in weakness.

DECEPTIVE DESIRES

In all of this, we must pray that the Body of Christ would understand the precise characteristics of the Son of Man, who walked a short journey with his soul and body, but made camp in the Spirit. The campfire of the Lord is magnificent and holy, unable to be explained in finite language. Yet we must make Jesus' ways known.

Allowing lust and its relatives to reside in our members is not a wise choice to make. From my point of view and the understanding I have gained of lust, I know it will take people to places from which it will be impossible to return. I never drank alcohol or did drugs, but lust was my drug, and it was bad. Trouble after trouble marching slowly in a desert of counterfeit desires will kill us! Lust will always want more and more—*Just one more look* or *Just one more second.* Those thoughts are deceptions of the flesh and the devil. With his bow in hand, the enemy plays archery contests in our minds, seeing who will win—us or him.

For men, such troubles are many; but it's the Lord who delivers us out of them all (see Ps. 34:6). Earlier in the book, I mentioned briefly how to fight lewd thoughts and the intricacies that follow after. We men must take heed to these instructions for they are the life on the line for our souls.

ON SECOND THOUGHT

Jesus says that His sheep know His voice (see John 10:27). This is absolutely true. Thoughts are very translucent and vague at times, but mostly enlightening. Allow me to explain. Not every thought that invites itself into our mental souls is ours. Having discernment and wisdom, according to the Spirit of God, is very critical in the Christian life so that we can counterattack evil thoughts with the Word. When thoughts rise up into our minds, sometimes it's just us; at other times, it's our enemy with his fiery darts, causing us to be interrupted and disrupted in our thought process. The Bible talks about satan as having flaming or fiery darts, which cause burning and heated thoughts (see Eph. 6:16).

Let's say the thought was a negative one. We will always hear the right "thought voice"—the Holy Spirit—speak to us first. The Word tells us how to discern God's voice: *"For I know the thoughts that I think toward you, says the Lord, **thoughts of peace and not of evil, to give you a future and a hope"*** (Jer. 29:11 NKJV). Then the wrong one enters immediately after. But the second "thought voice" usually sounds much louder than the first. The second thought is always the one that wants us to do an act of evil or say something that is unfruitful and not acceptable in the ears of God or others. The second voice contradicts the first on a regular basis. As these thoughts go in and out of our minds, we need to discern them quickly and wisely. If they exalt themselves against the knowledge of God and His Word, we must cast them down immediately. In our world, we have seen hundreds, maybe thousands, of men and women, even children, act on their thoughts, and the results were clearly devastating.

I call the Bible "the greatest sleeping pill" because when we begin to read it, it purifies our minds from ungodly imagery, yet all of a sudden a spirit of slumber interrupts us, causing our bodies to yawn and feel tired. When this happens, rather than giving in, we must stand up and do a few jumping jacks or have a drink of water; we will feel refreshed and renewed (and we will see that it's just a spirit of slumber making us sleepy, not actual physical tiredness). Multitudes of believers in these last days can tell the difference—whether it's God or the devil talking to them.

Our "thought voices" are our own, and we must be scrupulous at all times. In essence, we have to be aware of the content of our thoughts and what kind of information is being deposited into us. We must know how to become one with God and hear His still small voice so that when the Shepherd speaks there is no confusion in the process. Prophets and prophetesses of God, like my wife, Michelle, hear the Holy Spirit's voice most of the time audibly on the outside and occasionally from the inside. It is not the same for everyone, but rarely does she feel impressed in her spirit when God speaks; usually she literally hears His still small voice, which is not my wife's own thought voice, and that is awesome! We must re-tune and quiet ourselves away from all the noise that surrounds us—the Lord will speak to us. This is what happened with the prophet Elijah:

> *Then He said, "Go out, and stand on the mountain before the Lord." And behold, the Lord passed by, and a great and strong wind tore into the mountains and broke the rocks in pieces before the Lord, but the Lord was not in the wind; and after the wind an earthquake, but the Lord was not in the earthquake; and after the earthquake a fire, but the Lord was not in the fire; and after the fire **a still small voice**. So it was, when Elijah heard it, that he wrapped his face in his mantle and went out*

*and stood in the entrance of the cave. **Suddenly a
voice came to him**, and said, "What are you doing
here, Elijah?"* (1 Kings 19:11-13 NKJV)

My wife and I are no different or better than anyone
else. We don't need a title in order to hear the awesome-
ness of His voice. One thing we do need is an ear to hear
what the Spirit is saying to the Church (see Rev. 3:22).
God is always speaking, yet He is not a blabbermouth. The
Great Architect desires to converse with His children, but
at the same time, the devil also wants to converse with his
children and the children of God. The devil uses our own
thought voices so we can be swindled, making it extremely
difficult for us to determine who is speaking to us. If the
devil used his supernatural voice, we would flip and go
crazy because of the way his voice would sound; it would
blow his cover and prevent us from implementing what he
instructed. This would frustrate his evil plans and reveal
his trickery. But if he can camouflage his voice with our
own voices (if we do not have discernment), it could open
a gateway of immeasurable evil in our lives; this is satan's
primary objective—deception.

Generally, most people, whether they serve the Lord
or not, do not have this kind of understanding in order
to detect pernicious thinking. Consequently, they follow
after and speak whatever enters their hearts; their thoughts
simply flow out of their mouths, which we call blurting,
offensive, and disrespectful speech. This can become dangerous for those who don't have close relationship with
Christ to know the difference between their own thoughts
and the enemy's voice.

Jesus said that out of the abundance of the heart the mouth will speak. *"A good man out of the good treasure of his heart brings forth good; and an evil man out of the evil treasure of his heart brings forth evil. For **out of the abundance of the heart his mouth speaks**"* (Luke 6:45 NKJV). In Proverbs it also says, *"For as he thinks in his heart, so is he..."* (Prov. 23:7 NKJV). We must be careful what thoughts we allow in our minds because they will determine our actions. If we dwell on and engage the enemy's evil imaginations, we will eventually obey his voice to our own demise.

NO RESPECT

Magnitudes of people around the world know firsthand what I am writing about. Satan is making sure we stay in a cloud of lustful cravings that can never be satisfied in order to bring us a zenith of disease and false dominance. Society and the world are always relating lust to sex, but it is also often associated with greed for power and control, though the general public tells us otherwise. This is a Jezebel spirit in its purest form under the influence of Belial, a demon general of satan's kingdom (see 1 Sam. 30:22; 1 Kings 21:13; 2 Cor. 6:15). Relationship with worldliness and distorted views is adopted by fools at such a great rate that it's beyond comprehension to the natural realm. Belial and Jezebel are interrelated. We cannot take part at all with darkness. Sadly, many are yoked in spiritual slavery and don't even know it. We know better; we are supposed to be a light in a dark place and salt in a world that has lost its flavor (see Matt. 5:13). In our day, unsaved people can't tell the world from a Christian, because we all look and sound alike. Distinct change and godliness has to be the attribute of all the people of God; we are called to come out from among them and be separate (see 2 Cor. 6:17).

To a certain degree we must become all things to all people to win some, that's very true (see 1 Cor. 9:22). Yet, we must do this with the *leading* of the Holy Spirit, adhering to His counsel at all times, not the counsel of our theological degrees and head knowledge of the Word. As a peculiar people and a holy nation, we must keep in mind that satan does not respect the Bible, esteem holy reverence, or worship God (like some Muslims believe). He knows the Bible better than we do, but does not respect it. When we only read the Word of God—apart from the Spirit—it is only words on a page; therefore, he does not respect the Word alone. He knows that the Kingdom of God is not in words, but in power (see 1 Cor. 4:20). The devil respects and gives reverence to the Holy Spirit! Combine believers with the Word *and* the Spirit of Christ who is in us—the hope of all glory (see Col. 1:27)—and *BAM*, satan will submit to our authority.

Until then, we must watch and pray and keep ourselves from idols (see 1 John 5:21). Idols can be anything we love more than God.

1. Children

2. Spouse

3. House

4. Car

5. Lust

6. Pornography

7. Ourselves

This is why we can't *always* become all things to all people. If I have idolized cars, I am deceived if I think I am buying a luxury car simply to "be all things to all people." No, I am just feeding my idol. Such thinking apart from the Spirit leaves room for error and confusion. As the Word says:

> *Do not be unequally yoked together with unbelievers. For what fellowship has righteousness with lawlessness? And what communion has light with darkness? And **what accord has Christ with Belial**? Or what part has a believer with an unbeliever?* (2 Corinthians 6:14-15 NKJV)

We must be careful at all times and not enter into situations without the Spirit of God ahead of us and with us. We have to walk in, walk with, and walk by the power of Christ's Spirit. There is no other way. The Bible says a great deal about idolatry and its consequences:

> *Certain men, **the children of Belial**, are gone out from among you, and have withdrawn the inhabitants of their city, saying, Let us go and serve other gods, which ye have not known; Then shalt thou enquire, and make search, and ask diligently; and, behold, if it be truth, and the thing certain, that such abomination is wrought among you; Thou shalt surely smite the inhabitants of that city with the edge of the sword, destroying it utterly,*

and all that is therein, and the cattle thereof, with the edge of the sword (Deuteronomy 13:13-15).

PROTECT THE SHEEP FROM FALSE DESIRES

Some pastors and ministers can tell the voice of the devil in a second, with no hesitation. Because they see that it is insidious and hurtful to their flocks, they will war and pray against that spirit to bring liberation. Since love and awareness rests on the mantle of their hearts (see Jer. 3:15), they also know firsthand that if some of their congregants have heard the real voice of our adversary (or if demons manifest from the spirit realm and physically touch these believers), fear will begin to surmount and deliverance must take place. Therefore, they will need the pastor, apostle, or elder to facilitate in overcoming any confusion and bringing understanding to that situation. I have a trained ear to know the distinction of the voice of God and the voice of the devil. We must know how to discern the voices to know if it's us, God, or the devil. Jesus said that His followers, His sheep, will know His voice and follow His voice rather than the voice of a stranger (the devil):

> *And when he putteth forth his own sheep, he goeth before them, and the sheep follow him: for they know his voice. And a stranger will they not follow, but will flee from him: for they know not the voice of strangers* (John 10:4-5).

> ***My sheep hear My voice,*** *and I know them, and they follow Me* (John 10:27 NKJV).

There are many voices in our world today; mostly, those voices bring nothing but turmoil and tragedy. We must listen for only the Voice that brings redemption and beauty for ashes (see Isa. 61:3).

PRAYER FOR GUIDANCE

Father, I pray that You will help me know the difference between You and the voices of the enemy, whether through people or from the supernatural. Help me to stay away from all types of fleshly lusts and evil desires of greed, wants, or control, which is rebellion and witchcraft that can cause me to fall away from You. Holy Spirit, I ask You in the name of Jesus, show me if there is anything in me that is not like You so I can repent and move forward. I thank You, God, that You have given me the authority to cast down wicked imaginations and to rebuke demonic activity of all sorts. I praise Your name for the goodness and mercy You have shown me! May I never take it for granted. I receive the guiding of the Holy Ghost to empower me like never before. In the matchless name of Jesus Christ, amen.

CHAPTER EIGHT

Purpose-Driven Worship

*Finally, brethren, whatever things are true,
whatever things are noble, whatever things are
just, whatever things are pure, whatever things
are lovely, whatever things are of good report, if
there is any virtue and if there is anything praise-
worthy—meditate on these things. The things,
which you learned and received and heard and
saw in me, these do, and the God of peace will be
with you.*
—PHILIPPIANS 4:8-9

A guidebook has been written, before any of us were
born or even thought of, to help unlock our true
purpose. Our inheritance has already been established
since the foundation of the world; we just have to walk into
it. The awesome thing about it is that God has made a
way and made a *promise plan* for our lives before creation

came into fruition. We are all unique in our own way and must never think less of ourselves, no matter the condition we're in.

You were the only one on His mind when you were created in your mother's womb, a one-on-one appointment. Since you are reading this, it proves that you want to know who you are and why you're here. Prepare yourself to explore your architectural blueprint in order to build a foundation of stability and ascend with purpose so that the amazing plan of God that has been set before you can flourish. Destiny is written all over the DNA of your spirit.

Here's my acronym for *purpose:*

Placed

Under His

Rest and

Purpose

Offering

Salvation for

Everyone

YOUR REASON FOR LIVING

Now that you know that the Lamb's Book of Life (see Rev. 20:15) has your name written therein, it is time for you to dive into the pool of purpose. Worship is already within you, whether you sense it or not. Even when you don't feel anointed, you are. Just when you think He has left, He hasn't. Realizing that the Messiah has come to give *you* a reason to live life to the fullest and in complete abundance is an awe-inspiring idea. Your ability to recognize your purpose and potential with full conviction and certainty is just the outer ring of something fresh and new that is ready to commence in your time.

Praise must flow through our veins, adoring God's movement in the Spirit. Worshiping God is a power that has been given to us to help us divide and conquer the enemy's attacks against us and those whom we are hoping to lead to Christ. According to the Word, if we do not have any *hope*, it makes our hearts sick, causing us to give up on life as a whole. *"Hope deferred makes the heart sick, but when the desire comes, it is a tree of life"* (Prov. 13:12 NKJV). This is why wholeness in Christ is so important. We have much to offer to the Body of Christ and the world; we must not give up, but keep on walking with fervor and a fire for God. If we do, we will see a change in our attitudes as well as in our ill situations.

MIND GAMES

The devil will always paint a picture of us in our own minds, making us feel like we are unimportant and like everyone we encounter detests us. He will push us to feel ostracized so that when our friends and family come around us, it will seem that no one enjoys our company. He will play mind games, discouraging our hope and faith to the point that we give up on everything. The goal of satan is very clear; he never uses new tactics. Like a game of chess, demonic intervention will downpour into our lives, qualifying us as weak targets. His playing field is in our minds. He longs to make us ignorant of who we are so that the fruit of Christ will not come to pass in our lives. His objective is to grab hold of our desire for righteousness, kill it, and smash it until there is none left. If he succeeds, the end result is that we will lose the will to go on. The wicked one knows whether we allow ourselves to keep moving ahead without turning back to our old sinful ways. If we are prone to turning back, he can prevent our spiritual trees from blossoming. Satan and his evil horde want us to stay in darkness, knowing that if we come to the light, we will begin to produce good fruit in abundance (custom-designed for ourselves) to be a blessing to others.

> *Even so, every good tree bears good fruit, but a bad tree bears bad fruit. A good tree cannot bear bad fruit, nor can a bad tree bear good fruit. Every tree that does not bear good fruit is cut down and thrown into the fire. Therefore by their fruits you will know them* (Matthew 7:17-20 NKJV).

> *For a good tree does not bear bad fruit, nor does a bad tree bear good fruit. For every tree is known by its own fruit. For men do not gather figs from thorns, nor do they gather grapes from a bramble bush* (Luke 6:43-44 NKJV).

PURPOSE-DRIVEN WORSHIP

Make it brighter wherever you are, exhibiting a true paradigm of being a man or woman of righteousness and perseverance, an example for others. Adulation toward God is a privilege beyond wonders, miracles, and human imagination—for in the same instance He inhabits your praises, for we are *spiritual Israel* (see Ps. 22:3). His presence is worth more than a thousand universes. His voice is still, and the calm, which follows after, burns on the inside of you as a wild fire with the fragrance of the breath of His presence. The firm vocals of rushing water resonates out of Him (see Rev. 1:15), exploding you into a different dimension of purpose and power unknown to the world you live in. Every time your heart beats, you feel His heart beat at the same time. When He whispers in your ear to instruct you, you can sense His breathing on your face. A sweet aroma of His love and majesty will surround you until you are consumed with His presence. True, deep worship happens when you are behind closed doors at home and no one is watching.

We must learn again to serenade Him and place everyone else on hold as we should. Living for Him with our voices, living for Him with our hands, living for Him with our feet, blesses His heart to the highest degree. Worshipping Him with every ounce and fiber of our being, as we were created to do, is saying we really love the fact that He exists for us alone. He is a personal Lord and Savior who is there for us, and we must thank Him always for saving our lives from the ill wills of society and shattering the hands of the devil off us.

When God exhales, it sparks and ignites the anointing residing in our spirits, enabling us to love others and the Lord with gladness and meekness in total submission. Sometimes we have to be still for us to encounter the Holy Ghost with our total being. As a result, honesty and sincerity must cascade onto those around us, especially those in the faith. He covers us with His wings of healing, and overcomes us with His shadow, giving us an advantage over the enemy and enabling us to fulfill our true purpose in our everyday lives. As it says in the Psalms:

He who dwells in the secret place of the Most High
*Shall **abide under the shadow** of the Almighty.*
I will say of the Lord, "He is My refuge and My
fortress; My God, in Him I will trust." Surely He
shall deliver you from the snare of the fowler and
from the perilous pestilence (Psalm 91:1-3 NKJV).

His grace will overflow, and His face will shine through us in the Light, which will pierce any darkness with eternal power and confidence. When the Holy Spirit begins to do that, we have walked into the front door of our true purpose in Christ; this will amplify purpose-driven worship. Now it is the time to push ahead into the promises of God for us, *"For **all the promises** of God in Him are Yes, and in Him Amen, to the glory of God through us"* (2 Cor. 1:20 NKJV).

COMPASSION TOWARD GOD

God is very compassionate and merciful. We must come to a point of truly becoming what He desires for us to be. Worship helps us become one with God, bringing us back to where we should've been. Vast numbers of people have forgotten what it's like when the Spirit of the Lord arrives and moves in the earth. He rides the wind with His voice, which He did in the Garden of Eden in the *cool of the day* (see Gen. 3:8 KJV). When this occurs, I believe healing takes place, many are made whole, blinded eyes begin to see, and the deaf ears open.

Allowing God to radiate in the center of our souls teaches us that His ways will permit us to prevail over the stresses and perplexities of life. Let's allow His will to reign in us for the remainder of our days. His compassion and mercy will overwhelm our storms without the slightest effort on His part, if only we will give in to Him. If we have burdensome loads to carry, we must not stray from Him when His hands are reaching down to us. He holds everything together by the Word of His power (see Heb.1:3). Let's revere the Lord and give Him praise, knowing He deserves it for the kindness He has shown us. He is a God who exemplifies a character of love, admiration, and a willingness to bring us up when we are downtrodden. The Rock of Ages has said time and time again that He is the very source of our strength when we feel exhausted from trying to overcome daily battles in our minds. We must go back and reduce ourselves in His presence and influence, which will enable us to counterattack the enemy with potency.

His tender mercies and great forgiveness will consistently restore us as His compassion takes residence in our circumstances. We have to regularly re-purify our embrace of oneness with the Lord. He is always in a position to receive our adoration.

Adonai is never in a specific mood one day and a different mood the next day, as if He was bi-polar. He always has open arms that are outstretched to make sure that we know He will always be there for us. So that we can understand Him more fully, He will sometimes have us maneuver in ways that can bring confusion—but this does not mean that He is confused or brings confusion since He is not the author of it (see 1 Cor. 14:33). However, He never shows us the big picture all at once. We cannot figure God out, but must give in and lean on His ways, showing the Lord that we are submissive, obedient, and patient enough to wait on Him. The ability to know our true purpose in life and to be aware of various ways the enemy tries to slip in will be simple if we submit to Christ wholeheartedly.

Letting our eyes wander in a distant gaze, enamored with different spirits and their impious movements and softness of touch, will slowly trap us in a cave of darkness and shame. God must reign always in our hearts and minds or the blessings will not come down from the Father of Lights (see Jas. 1:17). We must let our lives emanate His Wisdom—the Messiah who guides and embraces us at all times with the warmth of His precious Spirit. He is our salvation, our strength, and our deliverer. When we really need Him, He will always show up. His healing rain will fall on us once again to make us strong, even when we do not deserve it.

> But God, who is rich in mercy, because of His great love with which He loved us, even when we were dead in trespasses, made us alive together with Christ (by grace you have been saved), and raised us up together, and made us sit together in the heavenly places in Christ Jesus, that in the ages to come He might show the exceeding riches of His grace in His kindness toward us in Christ Jesus. For by grace you have been saved through faith, and that not of yourselves; it is the gift of God, not of works, lest anyone should boast (Ephesians 2:4-9 NKJV).

The entire world is going to experience and literally see that Jesus is alive and well in the very near future. Chains will be broken; lives will be healed in every area as long as we walk after His Spirit every day, for tomorrow is not promised to anyone.

A.S.K. GOD

Ask

Seek

Knock

Jesus said, *"Ask, and it will be given to you; seek, and you will find; knock, and it will be opened to you"* (Matt. 7:7 NKJV). His truth will make us free indeed, always and forever (see John 8:36). One aspect of our freedom is our ability to ask. Ask God for His holy kiss as we do toward others in the faith (see 1 Thess. 5:26; 1 Cor. 16:20). Ask God, "How are You feeling today?" Ask God, "What can I do for You today, Lord?" We're always asking Him to do things for us; why not ask God, "Daddy, what would You like me to do for you today?" or "What would You like me to do for someone else to be a blessing?" We must neglect spending time with our heavenly Father.

OVERPOWERED BY LOVE

Let's let His Hallelujah explode inside our members like a wild fire. Let's let the blaze of His Son's power fill us with goodness and burn in the depths of our bones, shut up in your members (see Jer. 20:9). Let's let God reign in our souls. His pillar cloud of fire in the Spirit will lead and overtake us, guiding us into a new day of restoration and peace like He once did with the children of Israel (see Exod. 13:21). Let the grown men fall onto their knees again, hugging themselves in the sight of God and individually declaring how much they have missed their Creator from their youth and how much they adore and love Him. Let's allow the Holy Spirit to become our hiding place and total fulfillment. When we draw closer as broken vessels, He can flow into and fill us spiritually all the days of our lives until we are old and feeble, ready to enter into the arms of eternity.

The Lord will make Himself strong in your weaknesses. Then you will be able to make an impact in the lives of others who are struggling and being hit with all kinds of situations. Let His truth raise you into an adult of integrity. Subsequently, you will be able to find yourself. Let His grace be greater than the whispers of condemnation within your own heart. You have been born again into a new image, the image of Christ, the Wonderful, who sits high and looks low (see Isa. 9:6). Allow the Counselor to counsel your mind with total transformation. Put your life in His hands. Let Him walk up and down in the midst of your heart so that when the Great Physician opens you up, He will see His Son's footprints of hosanna and mercy. He will bring you into a new place containing a heartbeat of holy love with His Son's imagery on the surface of your own spirit.

God is a veil of righteousness hovering in front of your vision, and when He speaks to you, the veil is removed so you may clearly see His holiness and majesty. Cherubim's and His Seraphim's yell with high-powered voices saying how majestic Adonai really is. When they see the veil removed from the eyes of humans, the heavens rejoice, and a warm chill will fall from the top of your head down to the depth of your being. Feeling His presence with flames of fire from His eyes will overcome you. His love is burning the souls and the ears of His people, causing them to return to Him. He is always preparing a place of new heights and healing for all people. Open your eyes to His wonders and worship. He fills you from on high, causing everyone to become jealous of you.

We look just like Him. We are an exact image in His Son (see Gen. 1:26 and 1 John 4:17). The Holy Spirit extends His glory and exhortations to the inner person, we must let Him do this. We must always position ourselves toward the center of truth and edification, honoring His commandments to the highest degree. Purity in worship is showing Him that we are available at all times to our God who *is* love. He doesn't have love; He is love. We must humble ourselves before His Holy Mountain. Let the prophets humble themselves; let the pastors fall to their knees; let the evangelists speak softly. Let every nation be still and fall prostrate in adoration of our Lord.

This is a small scenario of what it is like to be on familiar terms with the Lord in purpose-driven worship in our lives and for our lives. The result is spiritual enrichment, which comes by worshiping God with all of our existence.

LIVE LONG AND MAKE A DIFFERENCE

As we get older, we are supposed to get wiser in our lives, knowing that we don't have long to live on earth and desiring our years to mean something when it's time to move on to the next world. God never said that we would live 70 years or possibly 80. That was a prayer of Moses to God on the behalf of his dealings with the Lord and the children of Israel (see Ps. 90:10). God mentioned people's lifespan in Genesis 6:3, stating that humankind will live up to 120 years of age; this was the last time God declared how long people would live. This shows why some people all around the world are reaching the age of 118, which is no surprise to the believer who knows what the Living Letter declares. I believe Christians pass on and sinners pass away; God's heart of compassion, mercy, love, and faithfulness is such a small part of who He totally is as our Master and Lord. YES He will make sure we are absent from this body and present with Him forever! This is why worshiping Him in spirit and in pure truth is so important (see John 4:24). Having a heart of purpose-driven worship is so inspiring; it will move in the hearts and minds of the most vile of all creation. Let's worship and praise God the way King David did when he asked the Lord to give him a clean heart (see Ps. 51:10). This goes beyond dancing in the spirit. If we ask Him how to do it with a clean and pure heart, He will perform His Word in and around us.

PRAYER OF WORSHIP AND PRAISE

Ancient of Days, You are my oxygen when it becomes difficult to breathe. Be my strength from within my inner person when I am weak. You are my divan I rest on when weariness overcomes me. You are my water when the fire gets too hot. You are my hands when I can't hold on any longer. You are my feet when I can't move forward to bring good news because I am flooded with evil all around me. Lord, You are my eyes when I am sleeping, watching over me to make sure the enemy doesn't injure me. I worship You, Father, always and forever. I am amazed and in awe of Your presence in my life. The songs I sing, the tears I cry, and the yells I scream never fall on deaf ears. Oh, Father, how Your love reigns within me. You never forgot me when others abandoned me. You never condemned me when I fell away and came back because Your love and mercy were so influential and overpowering; surrender was the only solution. Thank You, Father, for Your endless and irresistible Love! In the name of Jesus, amen.

CHAPTER NINE

The Living Water

He who believes in Me, as the Scripture has said,
out of his heart will flow rivers of living water.
—JOHN 7:38 NASB

There is a big difference between sinners and saints. Sinners practice sin; Saints practice righteousness. When pianists practice piano and hit the wrong note, they don't continue hitting the wrong note. They go back and correct it, trying not to hit that key again. Therefore, they are practicing how to hit all the right things in order to reach perfection and success in the future. This is like the life of a saint—always reaching toward perfection. A sinner does not live like this. Sinners wallow in and practice sin every day. They don't repent or feel bad when they sin against themselves or anyone else. No, they look forward to doing it again, with no conviction in their spirits, especially if their consciences are seared, not unlike numerous believers (see 1 Tim. 4:2). They don't have the Holy Spirit correcting them, like saints do, before they do or say something wrong. Basically, they are doing what they are supposed to be doing as children of the enemy.

As I mentioned previously, the right "thought voice" comes into our minds first, and the second one, which is usually louder, comes afterward to deceive us to fall into a trap of despair. *Which one will we follow?* Most assuredly, many of us follow after the louder voice. Instead, our goal should be to become those who allow the Holy Ghost to arrest our spirits and take us captive. The apostle Paul said it best, asserting that he was a prisoner of the Lord Jesus Christ, sanctioning himself to be captured by the Master (see Eph. 3:1; Col. 4:3).

This is fundamental to understanding who the *Living Water* is. I have to reiterate this again because it is so important to the Christian—the sacrifice that was provided for all humans to receive as a free gift in turn *cost Christ everything*. When people live in rebellion against Christ, they are telling God that the ultimate sacrifice He made is meager and inconsequential. God gets offended when human beings reject His idea of sacrificing His only born Son. Such people are plainly spitting in His face, saying, "What You did for me was hollow and vain." Let's think about that for a moment. It is dreadful to even write or talk about, especially to the sinner and the backslider, when it comes to the offering of His only Son. We must be aware of the high cost the Lord had to endure, refusing to diminish its magnitude.

We must turn and change for the better, submitting to His will as we give up ours. We *all* were bought at a high price, and our lives are not our own! Many don't turn to the Messiah because they are angry with God or with people who have hurt them in the past. The past is inside of us. When people say to "leave things in the past," we can't really since the past dwells within us. This means we need to be free from something greater than ourselves, Thankfully, Christ Jesus can liberate us instantly, though sometimes He does it gradually. The point is, He will do it, no matter the wait. Will we allow patience to have its work in us so that we will become like Jesus? (See Jas. 1:4.)

If you are one who struggles with this—if someone has hurt you or if you are walking around at home, work, church, or any other place feeling angry—God wants to heal you right where you are hurting.

THE SPIRIT OF ANGER

Anger is a very strong spirit. Therapists believe anger is a very strong emotion. Although both are correct, there is a lesson to be learned here. I have dealt with anger on a great level. It caused me to be very bitter and unforgiving toward anyone who caused me to get upset or offended me. I used to feel the anger rise inside of the center of my belly and would give full vent to it. I became, as it says in the Book of Proverbs, a fool. *"A fool expresses all his emotions, but a wise person controls them"* (Prov. 29:11 GW). The Word also says, *"Do not hasten in your spirit to be angry, for anger rests in the bosom of fools"* (Eccles. 7:9 NKJV). There is no difference between fits of rage and furious anger.

It did not matter to me who you were; I would just blow up, even without much provocation. My family had to deal with this for a very long time. This fierceness took a toll on my heart and mind. I would start to think about things I previously never would have thought of in a bad situation. The greater the hurt, the greater the pain I wanted to inflict on the other person. Radical demonic thoughts of fury would pound on my mind as if I was a volcano waiting for just one more word or situation; I was always ready to explode! Just like God gets glory when we praise and honor Him, satan also gets his glory, praise, and honor through evil doing.

Anger is a spirit that can cause our destruction. The Bible says of anger, *"Make no friendship with an angry man, and with a furious man do not go, lest you learn his ways and **set a snare for your soul**"* (Prov. 22:24-25 NKJV). Anger for me is now an emotion; before, it was a spirit. We have to catch it; it is very critical that we do. Believe me, anger is not an emotion to play with; it is very serious. There were times when the anger was so bad I couldn't even keep my head together. I thank God that I now get angry in my head and not within my belly—as I used too, which I would feel deep down, rising on the inside, exploding me into an unknown person. It was terrible when that would happen. Then a spirit of control began to form in me and I followed different pathways that I didn't want to walk on, but I did anyway.

Fortunately, the Bible also tells us what to do with our anger. *"Be angry, and do not sin. Meditate within your heart on your bed, and be still"* (Ps. 4:4 NKJV). I had to learn to forgive and forget just like Jesus did for me. Forgetting was the part that became the hardest if I did not stay under the blood of reconciliation. I really did not want to forgive my enemies, my family, and my friends for what they had done to me. But the Lord intervened and said, "Son, you have done things to others that you have forgotten. Remember, I have already forgiven you for your sins against Me, so you are going to forgive others." When He spoke to me about forgiveness and letting go of the junk within myself, at first I rebelled, but as time went by, I yielded to His will so I could be made free.

Partaking from the Living Water and walking in a Spirit-persuaded mindset will always bring deliverance to those who run with fortitude for change in their lives. I advise anyone who deals with anger to go before the Holy Counselor and seek His guidance. I am living proof that He will set them free! *"Remember this, my dear brothers and sisters: Everyone...should not get angry easily"* (James 1:19 GW).

SIMILAR EXPERIENCE

Heaven is a real place. Hell is a real place. God doesn't send anyone to hell. They send themselves there by rejecting Christ (see Rom. 3:23; 6:23; 1 John 5:12). To the theologian, I understand that it is God who sends people there because of the power that He contains to send us. However, I am writing from a spiritual aspect with basic teaching for all believers. Thus, for the purpose of this book, we can say that each person who goes to hell makes that choice by denying God's offer of salvation.

Besides money (which is the subject of 2,084 verses in the Bible), hell is the second-most-discussed topic in the Bible. Why? God's desire is that we would not go there (see Matt. 25:41). It's a terrible place.

WHOSE SIDE ARE YOU ON?

Hell is not a place where people wait until they are good enough to go to Heaven; it is a real, tangible place, and it is eternal. Proverbs 8:36 says, *"...All who hate me, love death."* The Holy Spirit is not a God we can push to the side when things get out of hand. Somehow we must come to terms with and meet the Lord where He is. Communication has always been the key with God. Conformity as a living sacrifice is of utmost importance, along with pursuing all that the Lord has for us if we follow His examples. Sanctity must be the main objective for every Christian in order to ensure holiness. The Lord said that without holiness no one will see Him (see Heb. 12:14).

If you find yourself in a situation that is very hard to break out of, immediately get in contact with your apostle, bishop, or pastor—someone who will help you through your struggles and who walks in power, holiness, and strong deliverance. Staying in a situation that could lead you to a place of eternal misery and destruction is not worth losing your soul over.

Take into account the story of the rich man in Luke 16. (This is the parable of the rich man and Lazarus, not to be confused with the Lazarus who was raised from the dead.) Lazarus would beg at the home of the rich man, hoping for crumbs from the rich man's table so he could eat. But the rich man would not have mercy, and eventually Lazarus died and was taken to a place called Abraham's Bosom. After a while, the rich man died too. As he suffered in hades, he saw Lazarus in Abraham's Bosom, and he asked Abraham if Lazarus could dip his finger in water and cool the rich man's tongue. Abraham had this response:

> *Son, remember that in your lifetime you received your good things, and likewise Lazarus evil things;*

but now he is comforted and you are tormented.
And besides all this, between us and you there is
a great gulf fixed, so that those who want to pass
from here to you cannot, nor can those from there
pass to us (Luke 16:25-26 NKJV).

In this passage, Jesus revealed a spiritual secret of the unknown to us (see Deut. 29:29; Dan. 2:28; Isa. 45:3). Now we know without a shadow of a doubt that hell exists. The proper term in the New Testament is *hades*. Hades is not hell; this is just theologically being correct. For the sake of simplicity, we will speak of hades as being hell; they are similar, in that both places are hot. It is just easier to understand without all the breakdowns of derivatives and languages.

In Luke 16:23, the rich man lifted his eyes and saw Abraham and Lazarus afar off, enjoying the eternal comfort of God's paradise. A great *chasm,* meaning a deep opening like an abyss in the earth, separated them one from another. To his amazement, the rich man started yelling out to Abraham to give him water to cool his tongue because of the torment of fire and the eternal anguish he was suffering—but as we read above, this was not possible.

This story is incredible, mysterious, and frightening; the Lord's heart is not for anyone to go there. Nevertheless, millions everyday choose that path by dismissing the plan of redemption. According to statistics, 150 million people are born every year, and out of that number, only 150,000 give their lives to Christ. That's about ten percent; the rest remain lost. We must bring up those numbers quickly— Where are the evangelists? We need to work fast, all of us. Let's go out to the ghettos, the suburbs, the inner cities, everywhere, and let's go get them so that where we are, they can be also!

The world today and many Christians claim that America is a Christian nation. I say we are not a Christian nation. We used to be, but now we are a nation with Christians in it. We as Christians in this nation must come together so that we can have an encounter with the Living Water on a more unequivocal and vast scale—to refresh us who are already saved and in order to lead more souls into Heaven (see Prov. 11:30; Dan. 12:3; James 5:20). Sinners claim to believe, and they do right by believing in God; however, the devil also believes in God. What's it going to take for sinners to repent before death knocks on the doors of their hearts? The answer is they must realize they need a Savior for their souls to be redeemed. Sinners believe and so does the devil, but saints confess one to another to bring hope and healing.

GOD WILL NEVER DO THAT—OR WILL HE?

We are blessed that He has chosen us to bear His fruit and establish His Word throughout the entire planet (see John 15:16). The Lord revealed to me that He wouldn't save everyone—it's not that He *can't* save everyone, but that He has given us free will, leaving it up to the individual to say *yes* to His Son, Jesus, in order to be saved. I am fully aware of Calvinism's belief of predestination, but that is not the view here, and it is not a subject that I have room to discuss in depth. In simple terms, predestination causes people to believe that Christ will not save everyone because it's all predestined in His mind; He knows who will make it and who won't. Thus, in this line of thinking, if God needs to use someone to glorify Him, he causes a person to reject Him (such as Pharaoh in the days of Moses). God did say that He has mercy and compassion on whomever He wishes, that some are vessels for destruction and other for honor (see Rom. 9:1-23). If the Lord saved everyone, then who are the people Jesus is going to destroy at the end of the seven-year tribulation? (See Zech. 14:3; Joel 2:11, 31; and Rom. 12:19.) The Messiah is going to take vengeance on humans, those who rejected Him and lived a life of sin and rebellion. I know this might sound harsh, but it's in the Word.

Unfortunately, many Christians are ignorant to what the Bible proclaims about a lot of different subjects, including this one. Jesus said, *"Revenge is Mine, I shall repay"* (Heb. 10:30). On whom is He taking out His revenge? Sinners! Why would there be a White Throne Judgment if every single person got saved? (See Rev. 20:11-15.) It's up to each person to make that final decision before the curtain comes down and the show is over. This is evidence that there will be many people who decide to go the other way and do not make it to Heaven with us.

I believe the reason multitudes of Christians do not believe in a God who will do such things is the fact they never read the back of the Bible—the Book of Revelation, and pastors don't teach this book in Sunday school or from the podium as they should. I have studied and still study the Book of Revelation since 1987, and the scrolls, seals, and bowls of judgment are still the same today as they were thousands of years ago, as foretold by the apostle John. Whenever I speak to unbelievers or backslidden Christians, they constantly give me the excuse that they are busy. They are busy doing this, busy doing that, busy going here, and busy going there, especially on Sunday. They have all these justifiable reasons to avoid visiting the house of God. I have heard it so much that there is an acronym for it:

Being

Under

Satan's

Yoke

They may as well profess this to be a fact with all the defenses and excuses they use.

HARD TO HEAR

I know this might be tough to comprehend; it's a horrible thought to process. We have to realize that God is not just a God of love, but He is also a God of judgment and justice. We need to stop placing the Lord in a box. He can destroy a person if He wants to, creating another one just like that person. I'm not saying that God will do that, knowing full well that He desires for many to go to Heaven (see 2 Peter 3:9). It saddens His heart seeing sinners and backsliders by the millions every year going into hell. (In Isaiah 5:14 it declares, *"Therefore hell hath enlarged herself, and opened her mouth without measure: and their glory, and their multitude, and their pomp, and he that rejoiceth, shall descend into it."* Again, the Bible declares that hell is never full; it always wants more and more). We must not presume upon Father God and His mercy and grace; He is not a figurine to play with.

On the other side of the fence, thousands have rejected the love of the Son of Lights (see 1 John 5:11-12). We do not know who has chosen God according to their motives and intellect, making an empathetic decision within themselves; only God knows such things. But we can fervently push forward and diligently preach and teach the Gospel of Christ to every person, not knowing with complete assurance who is going to Heaven or not. I don't have a Heaven or hell to give to anyone, so I cannot judge anyone in who is going there unless the Lord reveals that to me; our responsibility is to make sure we get as many as we can into the Kingdom where Christ resides. So we must teach anyone who has an ear to hear, letting Adonai make that final verdict.

Until then, our lost family members need our prayers every day so the Lord can intervene on our behalf to dodge the possibility of our loved ones being placed in the center of hell's torment. Every day I ask God to save my two younger brothers, just like the rich man in Jesus' parable. In Luke 16, the rich man had five other brothers, and he begged that they would not to be where he was. He pled with Abraham to get him out of that anguish and torture of fire, which burned him all over his body and in the inner and outer parts of his soul with a worm that crawls and slithers in, around, and over all those who go there. *"Their worm does not die, and the fire is not quenched"* (Mark 9:48 NKJV).

I entreat all those who confess Christ from their lips, but whose hearts are far away from Him, to run from the possibility of becoming a fallen soul who will never again remember the great memories of family, friends, and this life, but will have the constant torment of, "I should've changed and listened when they told me about accepting

Jesus, but now it's too late for me." All those who go to hell will never hear the sound of birds chirping or see a beautiful sunset again. In hell, there are snakes of all sizes, spiders, pain, gnarling, regret, resentment, screaming, fire, torment, and eternal suffering. Also there is a darkness that can be felt, just like in the days of Pharaoh and Moses.

> Then the Lord said to Moses, "Stretch out your hand toward heaven, that there may be darkness over the land of Egypt, darkness which may even be felt" (Exodus 10:21 NKJV).

I implore anyone to make sure they surrender their lives over to Christ. By doing this you don't have to go to that place of torment and darkness. I encourage you to make sure today you pray the "prayer of salvation" which is in the appendix of this book so that the Holy Ghost can dwell deep down in the inner most part of your spirit. Moving forward in the Lord will be your best bet for the miracle of change to take place in and through your life. No more looking back to what you left behind, plus taking back what the enemy has stolen from you for so long. Thus, born-again believers must avoid at all costs going back to their old lives. Demonic spirits can't wait to enter into backsliders and possess their bodies. Instead, we must be possessed by the Holy Spirit, the Living Water. He is joy unspeakable! As the Bible says, "...Do not sorrow, for the joy of the Lord is your strength" (Neh. 8:10 NKJV). He is the Spirit of power, love, and a sound mind in every born-from-above Christian believer. As Paul wrote to Timothy, "For God has not given us a spirit of fear, but of power and of love and of a sound mind" (2 Tim. 1:7 NKJV).

Although these verses are written in the Bible from the Lord Himself with the hand of a man, there are people who just will not believe, regardless of the truth that has been spoken. However, the final truth is that there will be no unbelievers when death comes to receive them. The final certainty is that they are unable to come back and tell us that the next world, either Heaven or hell, actually does exist.

Occasionally, particular people are selected by God to pass over into the realm of the spirit, experiencing hell firsthand, and then returning to inform us of what they've seen. It was a blessing for me that I didn't have to enter a dead state in order to see satan for myself, knowing the silver cord from my body to my soul and spirit was not cut. According to Scripture, there is a silver cord that is attached to people when they have an out-of-body experience or an actual physical death when the Lord takes them to hell or Heaven (see Eccles. 12:6-7). Death is not the cessation of our lives. Death in the Holy Scriptures is separation from the earth shell, called the body (see 2 Cor. 5:8). Essentially, people who have these experiences then go back into their flesh—their bodies—until the Lord allows that silver cord to be cut. When it does get cut, the person is permanently deceased.

> Remember your Creator before the **silver cord** is loosed, or the golden bowl is broken, or the pitcher shattered at the fountain, or the wheel broken at the well. Then the **dust** [person] **will return to the earth** as it was, and **the spirit** [person] **will return to God** who gave it (Ecclesiastes 12:6-7 NKJV).

THE MESSIAH ON HIS THRONE

The passage about the Lord resting His feet on the earth as His footstool really came alive for me in 2003 (see Matt. 5:35). Like the apostle John (see Rev. 4:2), whether in the body or out of the body, I am not certain, I was caught up in the spirit, and I saw the Lord sitting on His throne in Heaven! He was Glorious—sitting high and looking low! His hair was a medium brown color, and I could see through His body (He was almost transparent, but at the same time, He had flesh and bones as the Scriptures proclaim, but glorified). *"Behold My hands and My feet, that it is I Myself* [Jesus]. *Handle Me and see, for a spirit does not have* **flesh and bones** *as you see I have"* (Luke 24:39 NKJV).

It's really difficult to explain what His skin and body looked like. He had a gold crown on His head, and inside of His crown were millions of the same gold crowns. Immediately I thought, *Wow! This* **is** *the King of kings! Praise God in the highest! Jesus is beautiful and magnificent.* The best way I can describe Him is His clothes were part of His skin. It was the same with the archangel standing near Him, whom I believe was Michael. He was at attention and ready to fight. The archangel was taller than the earth, maybe about 50,000 miles tall.

As I watched, the iron scepter that was in Jesus' right hand was elevated slowly and then—*Wham!* He slammed it down quickly against the southern part of the universe and into the southern part of the earth with tremendous power! It sounded like a thunder crack times a billion, yet, it was not deafening to my ears. As He stood up, He said in a stentorian voice, *"Judgment!"* I knew this judgment was after the seventh year of the tribulation period, which is known as the Second Coming of God's Messiah. The Lord showed me the future of all the wicked and their countries; they will be destroyed since the children of disobedience discarded the holy path of righteousness and repentance. They also abandoned the sacrifice of His Son and His Word by their disobedient conduct. This is one of many reasons why the Judgment of God is coming suddenly to the earth. We must be prepared to meet the Lord Jesus with fear and trembling.

Below I was trying to find a Scripture relating to the scepter that I saw in His right hand. As you can see, it is found in the Book of Genesis.

> ***The scepter*** *shall not depart from Judah, nor a lawgiver from between his feet, Until* ***Shiloh*** *[Jesus] comes; and to Him shall be the obedience of the people* (Genesis 49:10 NKJV).

Jesus looked to be about 100,000 miles tall! The universe became frightened and bowed before Him, but the earth rejoiced!

In a blink of an eye, I was violently taken back to my living room. That experience changed me. The fear of Jesus coming off His throne was immensely powerful—way beyond what we can ever imagine! His presence is fearful and very terrible! I am glad that I am on His side. I've experienced demonic fear like I have never known (I talk about that experience in Chapter Ten), but this surpasses anything conceivable. On a greater note, this kind of fear emitting from God's wrath and His verdict is tremendously intense and dreadful when a child of disobedience is under it. Believe me; we do not want to stand around on the left side with the "goats" when His final ruling is to be passed (see Matt. 25:33). His blazing, fear-inspiring eyes will pierce through our souls, passing the depths of our spirits in raw judgment with His refiner's fire.

I fell on my face and started to cry while worshiping the great God, Yahweh, King of unlimited power! Jesus is real! Everything waits for, asks permission from, submits to, and bows to Him. He doesn't have power; He *is* power! Power asks Jesus when to move! Unexplainable mysteries were given to me, along with secrets unspeakable. It has been difficult to comprehend, and yet I understand. At the same time, it is too complex to write down into the chapters of this book. Here are a few *small* and very *simple* examples of what I mean:

He said that He *is* "*the Forever.*" He communicated these words to me:

> *Son, I AM still expanding the universe so I could fit inside of it, since its creation, the universe is still a speck of air dust, trying to accommodate Me* (see 1 Kings 8:27).
>
> Luis, I AM forever! I AM three forevers, but one God.
>
> All things created work for Me and serve Me, even satan. I AM in control; he does what I say."
>
> I never had a father or mother; I AM!
>
> I AM never beneath; it doesn't exist.
>
> I speak "water," and waves come to all shores of the land in fear and submission.

I AM in the past, the present, and the future all in the same day because tomorrow never comes; it always is one day.

I move East, West, North, South in every direction at the same time; you can never fathom, and yet I move toward My children in one direction spiritually and physically hear their cry for My Son to save them!

I AM speaking to you now, also in your mother's womb, in the present as you live your life, and also the "you" in the future.

My Name transforms the broken, the hurting, and the guilty. I restore and break down. I never "Rise." "Rise" waits for Me to give it permission to do so.

Déjà vu's are given to show you predestination; you lived this life once before, and then I seal the secret in the vastness of time you were created to borrow.

I, the Resurrection, take the ashes of My children from all the scattered oceans and seas, and will put them back together again on My Day in a blink of an eye.

I don't know about you, but God is awesome and cannot be explained in human language. To me that is profound and ineffable. He has fire-flamed eyeballs in His eye sockets and an actual sword for a tongue! The Book of Revelation expounds on some of these things He revealed and spoke to me about (see Rev. 1:14, 16; 19:12, 15...). These were written just as encouragement. We serve a *gigantic, sizeless,* and *all-powerful God!* It's so hard to find the words to explain it.

When the Holy Spirit allowed me to see what was permissible, it amazed my entire being. The Scripture *is* true; the earth literally *is* His footstool (see Matt. 5:35)! Praise God!

DRAWN BY HIS SPIRIT

The Lord promised me new life and new life in full abundance (see John 10:10). One thing that many in the Body of Christ don't seem to understand is when we live in this "abundant life," more issues come our way. Jesus did promise us trials of fire and tribulations until our end comes, whether it is in death or the rapture (see 1 Cor. 15:52). In my own life, I didn't hear the Gospel message in my younger years until I turned 15 years old. As a small child, ever since I could remember, I would hear about a man named Jesus doing all these great and powerful works and saying the most wonderful things. It knocked me off my feet when, at 15 years of age, God allowed me to truly understand it for the first time. Occasionally, my spirit heard the Gospel message when I was a kid in church with my grandmother, but my soul didn't hear it.

Now I am aware of those impressions in my inner being and how God deals with us by His Spirit and influence. John 6:44, which declares that no one can come to Jesus unless God draws them, makes perfect sense if we really think about it. *"No man can come to Me, except the Father, which hath sent Me draw him..."* (John 6:44). In other words, we will not want Jesus at all until God tugs on our hearts by the Holy Spirit—no tug, no Jesus. When I really got this, like an explosion, comprehension entered my heart like never before, putting together what I have never clutched when others spoke about it. Even in our human nature, we are given the will to choose Christ once He begins to draw us by tugging at our hearts with His Spirit.

On the other side, we have the option to stay away from the call of the Lord, which a lot of people have chosen to do. Rather, they ignore His voice and choose a path that does not promise absolution for their sins. They could simply say yes to God and move forward for the King's Kingdom, making a harmful impact on satan's domain, but they chose to give into a reprobate mind instead. All those who deny Christ get a second chance in the great tribulation period, but redemption is certainly not guaranteed (see Rev. 2:10). Blessed are those in the first resurrection: *"Blessed and holy is he who has part in the first resurrection. Over such the second death has no power..."* (Rev. 20:6 NKJV). Our hope is for the Lord to draw our loved ones to say yes to the call of God on their lives, just like we did, so they can be saved and be with us in Heaven for eternity.

IN THE EYES OF GOD'S ANGEL'S

Not only does the enemy attack us in all unusual aspects in both the seen and the unseen realms, but also because of the call on our lives for ministry. He also hates the fact that we look just like God. *"And God said; Let Us make man in Our image, after Our likeness..."* (Gen. 1:26). This passage in Psalms gives us even further understanding:

> *What is man, that Thou art mindful of him? And the son of man, that Thou visitest him? For Thou hast made him but **little lower than God**, and crownest him with glory and honor* (Psalm 8:4-5 ASV).

In the original Hebrew text, the word *Elohim* should be translated as *God* (as it is in the ASV), not as *angels*, as we see in some versions. We are not created a little lower than the angels; the Bible *doesn't* say that angels look like God, but that *we do*. Instead, angels are described as flames of fire and ministering spirits (see Ps. 104:4). In the Book of Enoch, which is not considered Scripture, but is held in high regard and was quoted by Jude in the Bible, Uriel is one of the archangels alongside Michael. The name *Uriel* means "flame of fire." Angels were mystified when the Lord decided to create humans; they couldn't comprehend and were baffled by what a human was until we came into existence (see Ps. 8:4; 144:3).

HOLY SPIRIT, ARE YOU A PERSON?

In the world today, we will hear a lot of different opinions and beliefs about the Holy Spirit. Alongside Jesus, the Holy Spirit is next in line for verbal attacks. Millions believe He is an "It," a force; others believe He is a being of some sort, but not personal. What they fail to understand is that He is God, the third part of the trinity. Though the word *trinity* is not in the Bible, the Old Testament gives much evidence for a three-member Godhead (see Gen. 1:26; Col. 2:9; 1 John 5:8).

The Word clearly tells us who the Holy Spirit is. If we thirst, He converts Himself into "water" (see 1 John 5:6; Rev. 22:17). If we hunger, He transforms into "bread" (see John 6:35, 51). If we are lonely and afraid, He converts into "the Comforter" (see John 14:26). Like a gentle surgeon, He opens up our hearts and presents them to us exactly as they are. At first, it is uncomfortable and painful to see things we don't like about ourselves. However, we would not grow and mature if the Lord did not show us what we really look like. Looking into our own reflections will reveal what needs to be worked on in the deepest parts of ourselves in order to bring out the *greatness* lying dormant within us.

THE GENTLE SURGEON

If a man goes to a medical clinic for his yearly check up, and his personal doctor suggests that the patient must have open-heart surgery to receive an artificial one, presumably when surgery happens, they get rid of the old heart and replace it with a new one. Likewise, when sinners give their lives to the Lord, their old hearts are taken away, and they receive new ones. Not only are their spirits born again, but they also receive hearts that come from the *"living water"* of God, which is the Holy Ghost.

New believers are susceptible to all kinds of attacks if they are not astute. They must be careful to not return to their old hearts by turning their backs on the Lord by going back to their old lives again. For the reality that the unclean spirit which left the *believer* from the beginning, will return to see if the Spirit of God is still within that person. And when he sees that person empty with no Holy Ghost residing in the believer before he or she left God, this is when he will get seven others worse than himself to possess that person. For instance, if a medical patient who received his new heart came back to his doctor ten years later, asking for his old heart, his doctor would think his patient was crazy. Jesus made this very clear. He said that we all (before being born again) have evil spirits living inside of us. When Jesus'

Spirit enters in, the evil spirits leave for a season, but then return to see if we are still saved. If image-bearers backslide into a fallen state—they are no longer serving the Lord in obedience to His will—the evil spirits they had prior will go get seven others more wicked than themselves and will re-enter those people. For clarity referring to Christians who are born-again cannot be demonically possessed, as long as you remain saved with the Holy Spirit living within you, you cannot be. I will explain further as you keep reading.

> *When an unclean spirit goes out of a man, he goes through dry places, seeking rest, and finds none. Then he says, "I will return to my house from which I came." And when he comes, he finds it empty, swept, and put in order. Then he goes and takes with him seven other spirits more-wicked than himself, and they enter and dwell there; and the last state of that man is worse than the first. So shall it also be with this wicked generation* (Matthew 12:43-45 NKJV).

THE BIGGEST LOSER

As the days go by we tend to resist the Spirit of God on a lot of different levels. The *living water* I write about is the proof on the earth for all people to realize that there is a real spiritual battle going on in the supernatural. In the unseen world there is a constant battle over souls. Satan and his minions do not want humans entering into Heaven, but into the lake of fire with him for eternity. Furthermore, in my experience, I have seen demonic possession personally.

This is why we cannot stray from God but remain in complete obedience to the Spirit of the Lord.

Unclean spirits are waiting to enter into a believer who no longer desires to walk with God for various reasons. Many have been prophesied over and are so excited about being in the ministry that they forgot where they came from and who put them there, which was God beforehand. These kinds of people are so zealous about being catapulted before their time that they ended up hurting themselves and others. And a select few have become demonically possessed, unfortunately, becoming an entirely different person from the beginning of their ministry.

As Christians, we see very clearly and are no longer blind to the mayhem of the devil's onslaught; thus, we have to walk in conformity with the Holy Ghost. Fighting a defeated foe has to be done with wisdom. We cannot war with someone who is already defeated. As a nation of sanctified people, we battle flies with bazookas and crickets with rocket launchers. In my mind, I believe that is too much artillery for something so small and probably insignificant. We must prioritize ourselves to put our situations in perspective and balance. We must bring them to the throne room of God and fight ourselves to keep them there, especially if the situations or burdens are too heavy to carry. Walking away from certain tendencies that the enemy might throw at us, knowing those things could bring us some type of relief, is also wise.

All things considered, even though satan is the god of this world, he is the loser in all areas of our lives. The only way he isn't the biggest loser is if we give him the upper hand. We must not leave our spirits unguarded. And we must stop giving satan so much credit. Remember, it's not always the devil doing it; sometimes it's just you, and he intensifies what you already were thinking from the start.

*The **god of this world** has blinded the minds of those who don't believe. As a result, they don't see the light of the Good News about Christ's glory. It is Christ who is God's image* (2 Corinthians 4:4 GW).

CHRISTIANS CANNOT BE DEMON POSSESSED

Jesus clearly addressed the issue of whether or not Christians can be demon-possessed (see Mark 3:27; Luke 11:21; 2 Tim. 1:7). He did not give us His Spirit who is weak and feeble! The Holy Word doesn't validate that people who are born from above, with the Holy Spirit living on the inside of their spirits, can become demon possessed. Christ desires everyone to know that the Living Water is not susceptible to satan at any given time. When born-again Christians have the Spirit of the Lord dwelling on the inside of their human spirits, the devil and his legions, princes, and generals do not have the power to come into believers and take the Holy Spirit out of their bodies whenever they feel like it. This would contradict the Scripture stating that the Holy Spirit in us is greater than the one who is in the world—satan, who is the god of this world (see 2 Cor. 4:4).

God's Word cannot come to fullness in our reality if Christ in us is *not* the hope of glory (see Col. 1:27) or if He has less power than our enemy. I believe Christians can be repressed, suppressed, depressed, or oppressed, but *not* possessed. If believers were to be possessed, to some degree, it would be because of their disobedience and willingness to fall away (see Jude 24).

Many believe true born-again Christians can be demon possessed because they have trusted their eyes more than what is written in God's Holy Word. Leaders teach this because they have trusted their eyes instead of the Word—believing what they have seen from the great liar and false wonder, satan, over what Almighty God has already established. What is already printed in the Bible is greater then what is seen. The Word of God is clear:

> *But if I, by the finger of God, send out evil spirits, then the kingdom of God has overtaken you. When the strong man armed keeps watch over his house, then his goods are safe: But when one who is stronger makes an attack on him and overcomes him, he takes away his instruments of war, in which he had put his faith, and makes division of his goods. He who is not with me is against me, and he who will not give me help in getting people together is driving them away. The unclean spirit, when he has gone out of a man, goes through dry places, looking for rest; and when he does not get it, he says, I will go back to my house from which I came. And when he comes, he sees that it has been made fair and clean. Then he goes and gets seven other spirits more evil than himself, and they go in, and take their places there: and the last condition of that man is worse than the first* (Luke 11:20-26 BBE).

This process will not occur if believers are doing right in the sight of God, but only if they begin dabbling in continual and unrepentant sin. If they do this, they open the door for the Spirit of God to leave; therefore, the unclean spirits can return back to their original hosts. Fortunately, *"...greater is He that is in you, than he that is in the world"* (1 John 4:4). We must live by the Word and stand by the Word at all times, refusing to let our guard down!

Here are some passages from Scripture that demonstrate the incredible power of the Spirit who lives within us:

> *And the Spirit of the Lord came mightily upon him, and he tore the lion apart...* (Judges 14:6 NKJV).

> *Behold, I send the Promise of My Father upon you; but tarry in the city of Jerusalem until you are endued with power from on high* (Luke 24:49 NKJV).

> *That He would grant you, according to the riches of His glory, to be strengthened with might by His Spirit in the inner man...* (Ephesians 3:16).

> *For our gospel did not come to you in word only, but also in power, and in the Holy Spirit and in much assurance, as you know what kind of men we were among you for your sake* (1 Thessalonians 1:5 NKJV).

> *For God has not given us a spirit of fear, but of power and of love and of a sound mind* (2 Timothy 1:7 NKJV).

We must stand strong in Christ by the supreme power of the Holy Ghost. If we do, He will never allow us to stay comfortless. In our times of need, He shows Himself strong. Let us always retain a thirst for the *living water*—the Holy Spirit.

PRAYER

Abba Father, reign over me. Increase the gifts that you have instilled in me since birth. Let greatness flood over me. Overwhelm me with Your love Lord. Let compassion be a 'beacon of light' for the hopeless and the dying; flowing from my life into theirs. Allow the Living Water to run through me pouring into empty vessels who don't know you intimately. I pray that they would see Christ in me the Hope of Glory! I need to be molded and fashioned after You, my Savior and God. There isn't anything else in this life that is worth more than You and Your awesome presence. Let me hear Your voice my Father, that I may continue the work You have called me to do. King of the Universe, I am here waiting on You, eternally grateful of Your kindness. Transformation is going to take place in my family because I know You. I pray Psalms 91 over my family now in the name of Jesus. Salvation will overtake my family according to Acts 16:31. I thank you in advance Father God for being so faithful and merciful to me. In the mighty name of Jesus, I pray this prayer with faith believing in You and that all I have prayed is done. Amen....

CHAPTER TEN

Can the Real Christian Please Stand Up?

*Hypocrite! First remove the plank from your own
eye, and then you will see clearly to remove the
speck from your brother's eye.*

—MATTHEW 7:5 NASB

In November 2002, on a cold Saturday night, I was sitting in my living room reading my Bible. It was already late, and the children were sleeping in their bedroom. My wife kissed me goodnight and decided to go to bed before me in order to have enough rest for the church service the next morning. I paused for a moment from reading and checked the back door of the house to make sure it was locked. When I came back from making sure the back door was locked, my wife had already entered the bedroom and closed the door behind her. Returning to the living room, I continued reading where I left off. While I was reading, an overwhelming feeling came over me, making me feel drained, tired, and sleepy. For some reason, the Spirit of God kept pushing me to continue reading, and I noticed that it was 1:50 A.M. Exhausted as I was, I knew to pray before I became too sleepy and was unable to pray to the Lord. I remember turning off the table lamp and laying back. A few seconds went by while I was praying, lying on my back with my right arm over my eyes. Suddenly I saw myself sitting up again. I fell asleep. As I sat up away from the couch, I saw a body stiff as a mannequin lying down on the sofa in the same position with my right arm over my eyes.

Being dead or separated from my body felt more real than this life. It felt so unusual; my senses were heightening by the minute, to the extent that I was able to hear a whisper of someone speaking in the country of Australia from my home in New York. I could feel the atmosphere and the air moving in me and through me. My soul was able to touch the walls and the air itself without me literally touching it. About that time I was in awe, captivated that my five senses had become seven and were magnified 50,000 times over! If I wanted to go through the ceiling or through the floor, I knew I had that power. Traveling at the speed of thought was pure normalcy.

Great distance is not an issue in the spirit realm, and eternity is understood in its fullness. I have to paint a mental picture for you in words to give you an idea of how long eternity is in our finite minds, knowing the human mind will never be able to comprehend the endless.

HOW LONG IS ETERNITY?

While this was going on, I comprehended what eternity feels like. Oh my goodness! We have not a centimeter of a clue how long infinity is. We don't understand eternity in these mortal bodies, but we come to *full* understanding of what it feels like when we are out of our earthen vessel. It is a very, very long and endless perpetuity; time is no more.

I will illustrate with a mental image to help broaden the perspective of endless duration the best I can. Let's say the whole earth is a planet of just ocean, just a large humongous mass of pure ocean many miles deep. And there is a small finch that must fly every one trillion years across our known universe, flying through countless galaxies to earth, and when the small finch gets to earth, there is a small piece of land he stands on to have a little drop of water, and then he flies back to his original destination. Now this little bird will continuously do this until he drinks the very last drop of the entire planet's water supply, and that is when eternity begins. This is the best mental picture I could think of to explain the enormity of eternity. That is a long time to fathom.

UNINVITED VISITOR

Realizing that my wife was in the room sleeping and so were the kids, I was not afraid and knew they were safe. As I was turning around, about 180 degrees to my left, I saw a huge, tall, dark, black figure about 12 feet from me, just standing there in half—half of his body was visible and the other half was inside the wall. He was the blackest of the blackest you can ever imagine! You can be in the darkest room with a blindfold and your hands over your eyes, but it would not be dark or black enough. I could feel his darkness! I was petrified; the fear was indescribable and horrific. It reminded me of Moses when God used him to manifest His wonders in Egypt and the Bible mentions that the plague of darkness could be felt. I believe this was similar.

> *Then the Lord said to Moses, "Stretch out your hand toward heaven, that there may be darkness over the land of Egypt, darkness which may even be felt." So Moses stretched out his hand toward heaven, and there was thick darkness in all the land of Egypt three days* (Exodus 10:21-22 NKJV).

The fear that emanated from this dark figure was unexplainable. If I took all the fears I have ever experienced, combined with all the fears of the world, and magnifying it 1,000 times, it still would not match the fear that came from this thing. I was forced to keep my eyes on him. He was hurting my vision because I could touch his fear with my eyes! I felt so afraid! But the fear did not enter into me. Yet, I felt my senses tremble. The fear of the Lord was more powerful inside me compared to the fear of the enemy.

Before I had a chance to think, the voice of the Holy Spirit inside of me whispered, "That's him, that's satan." Sarcastically I thought, *Oh...great!* Immediately, satan began to speak in a language I had never heard before. The words he spoke were not of this earth. I heard him speak into my left ear only. I just wanted this to stop. It sounded like evil gibberish, like he was blaming me for something. He was pointing toward me, yet not moving. He didn't have human fingers, but a black and dark human-figured body. I couldn't understand it. I was prevented from understanding "the language of evil spirits" in order to keep me safe and protected.

THE UNEXPLAINABLE

A strong feeling of hatred came from him, and I realized that he really hated me. I am speaking about a profound hatred not known to humanity. If I were to translate it into words, it would be something like, "I hate you. Get out of my line of attacks. You are hindering me." At that moment, he begins to get closer, and the closer he got, the weaker I became, and the more the evil in the room intensified! His voice, hatred, anger, and accusations became stronger and louder. As he kept moving, floating closer to me, something like electricity from every area of my body started to shoot out from within me to the outside of my spirit. (I apologize, but it's really difficult to explain the supernatural in earthly language.) Even as the electricity started pulsating from the inside of me outwardly, satan moved back quickly, like he was losing power and strength. Next, he quickly raised his right arm, and I was violently sent back into my body. When it happened, I saw my *"breath of life"* return to me. My soul and spirit sat up first, and my body followed after, and then *we* (body, soul, spirit) were one again (see 1 Thess. 5:23).

I began to yell at the top of my voice. "Help Me! Help Me!" As soon as I came to myself, praying was the first thing that popped into my mind. I started rebuking satan by telling him he had no right to show himself to me.

My wife was startled out of her sleep with all the commotion going on. She pushed the bedroom door open really fast, and it hit against the wall, *BAM!* She began to shout, "Honey, honey, what's wrong? Talk to me; you're scaring me. What happened?"

Although she was speaking, I was speechless. I couldn't talk, but prayed while rocking back and forth on the couch in the living room. I whispered to myself prayers to fight against the fear I had felt and the evil that was with me. It was 2:50 A.M. This occurrence kept its peak for about 25 minutes, but it literally felt like 20 seconds. Because I was not able to really hear anyone but myself praying, my wife just sat next to me holding me and comforting me until peace ruled me. Frantically, I tried calling my friends for counsel, but I just couldn't grab hold of the phone. It kept falling out of my hands from all the shaking. Everything around me was fading away. Eventually, the Lord touched my spirit and told me to be peaceful, and after that I was able to explain the event to my wife.

REVELATION OF EVIL DOMINION COUNTER-POWERS

The Holy Spirit revealed to me aspects of the demonic realm and power structure. As we all know, demons, devils, and evil spirits have names, ranks, sizes, and functions in chaotic order under the influence of satan, who has the spirit of the devil. Satan has generals and powers of the air at work for him.

When I was taken out of my body, and satan himself came to visit me, I was given understanding about certain names and some may not be in Scripture (I called this

262

revelation knowledge). So I will try my best to give you biblical passages to help understand my experience better. Here are the names of some of the more prominent evil spirits (you may be familiar with some of these): Belial (see 1 Sam. 25:17), Onokian (a general who hovers over Iran), Azazel goat (a goat-like demon, see Lev. 16:8-10), Spawn, Python (divination, see Acts 16), Oni, Beelzebub (see Matt. 12:24), Octopus, Guile (see Ps. 55:11), Leviathan (see Isa. 27:1, general devils/demons), Cormorant (see Isa. 34:11), Uzza, Azzael, Marine-water spirits (see Ps. 74:13; Matt. 8:32), animalistic spirits, the screeching owl (see Isa. 34:14, 15), spirit of Pan (Pan causes humans to have panic attacks), foul spirits, unclean spirits, wicked spirits, infirmity spirits (see 2 chron. 33:6), and countless others. They are in the hundreds of millions! We do not want to see these spirits or be confronted by them! These are principalities, powers, and rulers in high places and on the earth (see Eph. 6:12). Satan's kingdom is in the second heaven.

Whether people are unsaved or saved, these spirits will manifest and harass. If the devil was not bothering me at all, I would consider my walk with Christ and make sure that it is a genuine and legitimate walk. If we are not doing anything to put a spiritual dent into the kingdom of darkness, then something is wrong. If we are living as real Christians, by our very nature we will be a threat to satan's kingdom, which will cause him to go into an uproar.

Often, when people experience a foul stench in their homes, maybe in the bedroom or the living room, they first think that someone must have eaten something that did not fall right in the stomach. Probably one of the kids or someone else used the bathroom, or the garbage wasn't thrown out, or maybe something is cooking that doesn't have a pleasant scent. These are all legitimate reasons for such odors. But sometimes bad smells manifest when we know the plumbing pipes of the toilet are not busted—it is the rulers of this dark world. This is when we need to be courageous and, walking in the Spirit's power, stand up to these supernatural spirits, because we are being visited. The stench of demons is so foul it's like rotting flesh and feces burning at the same time, but this a foul-smelling spirit that comes out of hell from the center of the earth.

Principalities and Powers in high places are wicked beings that come from the second heaven. Many years before my encounter with satan, I had an experience with the demonic, though at that time I knew very little about the supernatural. At that time, I had a roommate, Alexci, who was a born-again Christian. He and I would always make it a priority after work to get into the Word and have a Bible study or go to mid-week service together. One day, I came home late from work, and as I was entering the front door, Alexci told me frantically that we needed to pray that very moment. He sounded a little freaked-out.

I asked him, "What's going on? Are you OK?"

He said, "No, I am not OK! I never witnessed something like this before."

I replied, "Witness what? What happened to you?"

(*Stammering*) He answered, "When I entered my bedroom to place my books on the table and walk toward the bed, the room temperature went completely cold like it was the middle of winter."

(*Slowly*) I responded, "Reeeaaally?" I knew he was a new believer and thought maybe he was joking with me, but as he went on, I could tell from his body language that he was telling me the truth. He was really frightened and confused about the whole matter.

He continued, "Luis, I know you taught me about what the Bible says about demonic realms and evil spirits and all of those crazy things, but I didn't think any of it was real. Man, I was able to see my breath it was so cold Lou, like it was 5 degrees in here. What really freaked me out was the fact that only my room was that cold, and just 3 feet from my bedroom door. I could step into the living room and it was hot, and so was your room!"

I replied, "Alexci, what did you do?"

Alexci responded authoritatively, "Well, I felt heaviness in the room and knew that these cold spirits were lingering with me. I had an overwhelming presence of fear and evil surrounding me, so I stomped my right foot on the floor as hard as I could and said in a loud voice, 'In the name of Jesus, I rebuke you demons of hell! Go back to where you came from! You don't belong in my house! My home is the house of my God!'"

When he stomped on the floor and rebuked the spirits that were in his room, he believed they went back from whence they came, and the temperature gradually returned to normal. If it had been the middle of winter, I would have thought nothing of it, guessing he might have left his window open. But this occurred in the middle of July. It was 84 degrees, hot, and humid.

I didn't understand until later on in my walk what the difference was between common foul spirits and what happens when rooms get cold as demons visit people. Now I know that when people experience something similar or have a shared experience with someone else at this level or greater, they have been visited by a principality in *high places*—the *high place* is the second heaven, which we call outer space, which is negative 463 degrees below zero. That is beyond what we know about how cold freezing is; it is incomprehensible. Car gas freezes at negative 150 degrees; imagine that for a moment compared to outer space.

When these evil principality spirits come down to earth (they roam up and down from earth to the heavens), as they travel, asking permission to accuse and harass us, they adapt to our environment. When they visit humans, they can also affect the environment around them, causing it to fit their desires and leaving a residue where they've been.

CAREFUL WITH ASSUMPTION

Let's return to the previous story of my encounter with satan. After a few minutes went by, I was able to explain the whole thing to my wife. The kids did not wake up at all during this whole time while I was explaining the situation. The whole ordeal was indescribable. Not one atheist, agnostic, unbeliever, or backslider in the world could have gone through what happened to me and continue to doubt that God or the devil exists. When I tried to explain this account to several people, most would say it was only a figment of my imagination and that none of it was real; it was all in my head and just a nightmare. These people presupposed that something was wrong with me. Not everyone understands the supernatural and why things happen to them or someone they know. As humans, we tend to label everything, and stay away from the unknown. If I wasn't a real Holy Ghost-filled Christian, I believe satan would have done a lot more damage than I could ever imagine.

As I mentioned earlier, when Jesus asked His disciples, "Who do you say, that I am?" Jesus discerned that His character was being questioned (see Luke 9:20). The religious people of that day did not understand the call on His life and who He really was. They condemned the Lord because of the unfamiliar and labeled Him as the son of a known carpenter, instead of the Son of God (see John 6:42). If they had taken the time to understand Jesus, they would have known that Jesus was the "child that's born," who is the Son of man, and that Christ is the "son given," who is the Son of God. Alas, it never turned out that way for them, because their focus was on humanity. But it did work out for our good so we can have the opportunity to enter Heaven. We must be cautious in all instances, knowing the devil is always at work and never sleeps since he's a spirit, like the Spirit of Christ (but one will always be in our favor, and the other will not). Not all will accept who we are. The question is, are we able to stand when our reputation is judged? Will we stand for Christ and not be ashamed as many of His followers have done in times past?

Just as happened with Jesus, we will be judged and talked about for unusual things. It's up to us to hold on to what God has put in front of us with a fire that never dwindles, whether we have had visions or dreams or experiences. We must keep walking into the destiny that was hand-painted and sculpted for our lives. We will be misunderstood at times and condemned for things that are not in our control, but we must hold on with hope, faith, and trust in the Lord with much prayer! In my life, this experience happened just a little while after I accepted the call of God on my life. *Easy* is not the word to describe the entire walk of an image-bearer, but it's possible for us to walk with the power of the Spirit as we listen to His voice continually. Satan will try to prevent and slow us down, but he can prevent us only if we listen to his voice and reject the voice of the Spirit of God. Satan knows damage will come to his kingdom if we are aware of who we are in Jesus.

THE WORLD'S COUNTING ON US

Hopefully, God's Word helps you and those you know to stay in obedience. My heart aches when I think about the billions of people who will not make it into Heaven. Billions in false religions and secular humanism are open-minded for all different kinds of methods and ideologies to get to God. There are 1.5 billion Muslims, 1.5 billion Catholics, 376 million Buddhists, 900 million Hindu's, 18 million Jehovah Witnesses, and 11 million Mormons. That is an enormous community who are deceived into believing a lie. There are 2.1 billion professing protestant Christians today, but out of this vast number, only 684 million are professing to be born-again, according to statistics.

Here's a basic background on these false religions that I've mentioned:

- *Islam*—believes that Jesus is only a prophet, a good man, and not God incarnate or the Son of God. Allah does not have a son, according to the Qu'ran. (See Proverbs 30:4; 1 John. 4:1-6; 2 John 7-11.) There is a major difference between the Elijah Muhammad that the Nation of Islam teaches as being the last prophet in the '60s and the Mohammad from seventh century Arabia. In my short period of being Muslim, I realized the two did not agree with each other about a lot of things.

- *Catholicism*—believes that works can get us to Heaven and that we can pray to the Virgin Mary to get to Jesus. In recent years, I heard over Christian radio a well-known pastor state that the Vatican received 4.1 million petitions to make Mary part of the trinity. (See 1 Timothy 2:5.) In Latin, *vatis* means "divine" or "prophetic" and *can* means "serpent" or "snake." Thus, *Vatican* translates as "divine prophetic serpent and snake." Idol worshipers are an abomination to the Lord, and we must be very meticulous in how we handle ourselves accordingly.

- *Jehovah Witness*—don't believe in Heaven or hell. They believe there is no Holy Spirit living inside believers. The Holy Spirit is just a force. Michael and Jesus are created beings. Jesus is not God, but *a* Son of God. He is *"a* Word," not *"the* Word." (See John 1:1; 3:3-8; Revelation 3:20.)

- *Mormons*—baptize their members in the name of the dead. They believe that their church has a group of men and women in the "spirit world" who are spreading the Mormon Gospel to the dead who have not received an opportunity to convert to Mormonism. And when people do say *yes* to this conversion, they also are baptized in the name of the dead. (See Matthew 28:19; Acts 2:38.)

Fallen souls with a fallen ministry who are living in a fallen world with a fallen mentality will cause us to fall many times. Here's what the apostle Paul wrote about how easily we can be deceived:

> *I marvel that you are turning away so soon from Him who called you in the grace of Christ, to a different gospel, which is not another; but there are some who trouble you and want to pervert the gospel of Christ. But even if we, or an angel from heaven, preach any other gospel to you than what we have preached to you, let him be accursed. As we have said before, so now I say again, if anyone preaches any other gospel to you than what you have received, let him be accursed. For do I now persuade men, or God? Or do I seek to please men? For if I still pleased men, I would not be a bondservant of Christ. But I make known to you, brethren that the gospel, which was preached by me, is not according to man. For I neither received it from man, nor was I taught it, but it came through the revelation of Jesus Christ* (Galatians 1:6-12 NKJV).

STAND FOR HOLINESS

If we claim to be real Christians who love God with all of our hearts, then we must stand up and proclaim the Good

News from the housetops and let everyone know that Jesus is Lord! Helping and assisting others to prepare themselves for the coming King is our primary objective. Only one way can get us ready for the presence of Almighty God, and that is having an attitude of repentance. Repentance is the key to eternal life. My prayer is that we will always allow the love of God and the certainty of His Word to resonate with love, true worship, forgiveness, obedience, and repentance in our mortal bodies and souls. Then the Spirit can truly live in us and through us and give God the worship that He rightly deserves. We just have to get back up and not stay in our bad situations. We have to keep on keeping on—never giving up knowing that God will never give up on us! Let's take a stand! Here's some encouragement from the Word about the importance of standing strong in God:

> *Draw near to God and He will draw near to you* (James 4:8 NKJV).

> ***Stand fast*** *therefore in the liberty by which Christ has made us free, and do not be entangled again with a yoke of bondage* (Galatians 5:1 NKJV).

> *Put on the whole armor of God, that you may be able to* ***stand*** *against the wiles of the devil* (Ephesians 6:11 NKJV).

> *Therefore take up the whole armor of God, that you may be able to* ***withstand*** *in the evil day, and having done all, to stand.* ***Stand therefore***, *having girded your waist with truth, having put*

on the breastplate of righteousness (Ephesians 6:13-14 NKJV).

*...So **stand fast** in the Lord, beloved* (Philippians 4:1 NKJV).

*Therefore, brethren, **stand fast** and hold the traditions, which you were taught, whether by word or our epistle. Now may our Lord Jesus Christ Himself, and our God and Father, who has loved us and given us everlasting consolation and good hope by grace* (2 Thessalonians 2:15-16 NKJV).

MAKE A STAND AND GET INVOLVED

To live under the shadow of the Almighty is an exciting journey (see Ps. 91:1-2). However, this journey will be short if we don't have the necessary tools to consistently be itinerant with the Lord, to help us build that one-on-one relationship with Him in order to see the blessings and promises manifest.

Saints who don't pray and seek after God as they should are carnal Christians. Never walking in the spirit, they are wondering what is going on, complaining to their spouses and friends: "Why are the blessings of God trickling in instead of raining in like everybody says?" Those who have trouble walking the walk of Life with Christ need to be more involved and learn to give themselves away. They must pay their tithes and offerings, give, and sow seed; they will watch God move mightily in their lives and finances! (See Mal. 3:8-10.)

One of many reasons why we have to pay our tithes is to break the back of this satanic stingy spirit that has a hold on many of us, preventing many from learning to become givers and not takers only. Multitudes of Christians do not have a problem paying out-of-pocket for worldly music concerts, all sorts of personal desires, high-priced restaurants, and various events. We must not be this way! Those who walk on this unruly path should get off quickly! In fact, the Lord God told me in regard to giving to His work and the Church, "Luis, My people could give their tithes and offerings to Me forever, and it will never amount to My giving of My only Son who died on the cross for you and for them!" We must learn to give not only money, but also to give our time away to others, as well as spending time with God—and God will spend time with us. "Give and it shall be given to you; keep and it shall be kept from you" (see Luke 6:38).

This law is for the singles and the married. In fact, singles and married couples should get connected and engage themselves in cell groups or ministries with their local church. We must be eager to find out if there are things we can do to serve the Lord and His people. We must serve our pastors, asking if we can be placed in positions that can help our pastors in the ministry or others in need—whether in the church or in out-reach ministry. There are thousands of people out there waiting on us, waiting to be blessed by our spiritual gifts. There are believers in the Body of Christ who can appreciate the anointing on our lives to bless and encourage others.

Also, many in the Church are struggling in their marriages. To those couples, I recommend seeking out marital counseling. Do not do this alone, particularly if you are single because of divorce. Assuredly, another couple in leadership, ordained by the pastor, who is stronger in the Lord than you, can come in and help mend the marriage by executing holy and righteous order. Always be accountable to your leaders, and you will go far in your walk with Christ and your marriage will prosper; the same will be true for the single people as well. If a single individual desires marriage they should always seek the Lord's counsel from either an apostle, pastor, or bishop. *"Beloved, I pray that you may prosper in all things and be in health, just as your soul prospers"* (3 John 1:2 NKJV).

SERVANTHOOD

There is nothing like people who know how to serve and submit under the Lord's shade. We do not have enough couples or single people going out there witnessing and helping the church and their leaders with ministry duties. This is our job; we are to work and occupy until Jesus' eminent return. Even though I am an apostle of the Lord Jesus Christ, I am a servant first. Titles we can do away with; there are times when these titles are important, but titles cannot be the sum total of people. If people don't know how to serve the Lord and those who inhabit the earth, they have much to learn. I am always striving to make sure I walk with a reputation in God's eyes as His friend. People in churches sing these songs to the Lord, clapping and shouting, I am a "friend of God," but He doesn't even know them. They must repent and examine themselves so God can come in and heal them where they hurt or where they lack in holiness, for without holiness no one will see the Lord (see Heb. 12:14).

STAND FOR PERFECTION

When we get involved in ministry, we will meet a lot of different and interesting people. As we stride for perfection in Christ and seek His face, we must be aware of who is in our loop of interest.

For example, if you are single, by no means should you go out alone with a person you like; that is just a snare and a trap. Be astute, keeping yourself from a position that could cause you to fall in sin. Be wise as a serpent and gentle as a dove, staying away from the appearance of evil (see 1 Thess. 5:22). If you do not follow the Word of God, you will lose yourself in the process, and then you will find excuses for why you are in that position to justify your means.

Ironically, there are multitudes of men and women in the Church whom we could minister to over and over again, yet no matter how simple the message is, it will never get across. Many times the Lord says that He will give them over to a reprobate mind if they continue in this manner. That's Bible, *not* Luis Lopez 101.

> *Let no one deceive you by any means;* ***for that Day*** ***will not come unless the falling away comes first,*** *and the man of sin is revealed, the son of perdition, who opposes and exalts himself above all that is called God or that is worshiped, so that he sits as God in the temple of God, showing himself that he is God. Do you not remember that when I was still with you I told you these things? And now you know what is restraining, that he may be revealed in his own time.* ***For the mystery of lawlessness*** ***is already at work*** *only He who now restrains*

275

will do so until He is taken out of the way. And then the lawless one will be revealed, whom the Lord will consume with the breath of His mouth and destroy with the brightness of His coming. **The coming of the lawless one is according to the working of satan, with all power, signs, and lying wonders,** *and with all unrighteous deception among those who perish, because they did not receive the love of the truth, that they might be saved.* **And for this reason God will send them strong delusion, that they should believe the lie, that they all may be condemned who did not believe the truth but had pleasure in unrighteousness** (2 Thessalonians 2:3-12 NKJV).

People can't constantly reject Jesus Christ and the finished work of the cross for years at a time and not go through much disorder and dissension. The adversary will not let up; he doesn't want these people to be saved or to repent from their backslidden state. Real liberty only exists in the arms of Christ, and satan's wicked agenda is making sure such ones are unable to find it. We must be very careful to never give in to a reprobate mentality, and in that way, God will prevent us from giving in to strong delusions in these final days we live in and so fulfill this prophecy. Today is the day of salvation for those who are lost or have fallen away—*come back before it's too late!*

If you are having difficulty being in Christ, or maybe you knew the Lord and have fallen away, go to a confidant you trust to help you be strong in God. An accountability partner will make certain you will not wane to the left or the right. No one is Jesus, Jr. The devil tries to deceive you in thinking you can do it all by yourself, transporting thoughts into you encouraging you to become isolated from everyone else. Remember that *isolation brings separation, but integration brings combination*. This is exactly what you need—to combine with other believers in agreement and put 10,000 to flight (see Deut. 32:30). Really, it's even more than that now because you have Jesus and are under the New Covenant of love and grace, so you have more authority. No matter who you are—single, married, or engaged—when you are broken and humble, you always know how to put your pride to the side and run after what is right in the sight of the Lord. The giving of *yourself* is important in the Body of Christ. It may not always be easy, but it is possible.

Typically, giving happens with our time, money, love and so forth, in accordance with God's will and plan for our destiny. The point is, we don't want to *inhabit a place* of always taking and not giving, becoming a reservoir and not a channel for blessings. There is a difference between receiving and taking in all relationships, especially in marriage. Think about that for a moment. When we are in need, we must sow. We reap what we give away (see 2 Cor. 9:6). We must stand strong in the Lord and follow after His Word.

Serving others brings humility and a joy beyond what our hearts can bear. A servant leader is a good leader. A lot of people want to lead, but no one ever wants to serve. (That is a head scratcher!) Let's keep together and walk in agreement with affection, especially with those of the house of the Lord. Why? Wolves hunt in packs, and they wait for the sheep to stray away alone. Then they attack and kill them, sometimes very slowly. When we push those who are on the fence, eventually they will fall off on the wrong side;

what they really need is that extra pull to the right side. If this doesn't happen, the evil one will come and take them away from the flock. Let's meditate on these truths from God's Word about the importance of sticking together as a Body:

> *Not forsaking the assembling of ourselves together, as is the manner of some, but exhorting one another, and so much the more as you see the Day approaching* (Hebrews 10:25 NKJV).

> *Can two walk together, except they be agreed?* (Amos 3:3)

> *For he who sows to his flesh will of the flesh reap corruption, but he who sows to the Spirit will of the Spirit reap everlasting life. And let us not grow weary while doing good, for in due season we shall reap if we do not lose heart. Therefore, as we have opportunity,* **let us do good to all**, *especially to those who are of the household of faith* (Galatians 6:8-10 NKJV).

STAND ON THE SURE WORD OF GOD

Years ago in mid-week Bible study the pastor taught that there are over 5,750 manuscripts written in relation to our world's history. The pastor declared that The Sacred Word is the most quoted of all, to the point that if we were to take all the Bible quotes from every book ever written and combine them, we would have the entire Old and New Testament, accept for 11 verses. Today, I don't know if that is totally accurate, but it sounded wonderful, which in my mind can prove beyond reason that the Bible is authentic as well as its author—God. There's no pretending that this Holy Book we follow is fake or altered, though some people say it is counterfeit. Such people walk in a spirit of error. We are standing on a sure word of prophecy and a very solid foundation. Peter said it best:

> *And so we have the prophetic word confirmed, which you do well to heed as a light that shines in a dark place, until the day dawns and the morning star rises in your hearts; knowing this first, that no prophecy of Scripture is of any private interpretation, for prophecy never came by the will of man, but holy men of God spoke as they were moved by the Holy Spirit* (2 Peter 1:19-21 NKJV).

STAND FOR HOPE

I named this chapter "Can the Real Christian Please Stand Up?" because a host of believers do not take God seriously and are not standing up for the Lord as they should because they are afraid. Jesus has done so much for humanity; we will never be able to pay Him back for what He has done. The only thing we can do is give our lives to Him completely, sacrificially, and obediently. We must stand through adversity, weathering storms with vigor in the direction of holiness. Without holiness, we will *not* see the Lord (see Heb. 12:14). We must stand fast when false religions begin to rise and try to contradict and tear down the Word for the truth it contains, while they are promoting a lie. Not all roads lead to Heaven, even though most

Christians think so. Four hundred times in the Bible it says that Jesus is the *only* living truth, way, and resurrection, giving life to all who believe in Him. We must recognize the words He spoke as pure and unadulterated truth. Jesus said, *"I am the way, the truth, and the life. No one comes to the Father except through Me"* (John 14:6 NKJV).

DATES DID NOT CHANGE FOR OTHERS

All religions work hard to make their way to God, but Jesus has already done the work for us to redeem us back to our Father. If other religions are so true in their ways, why do they accept each other? Many religious figures came and are now gone. Jesus Christ, the Son of God and the Son of man, died, causing the acknowledged timeline to change. Time is recorded based on the notations, B.C. (Before Christ) and A.D. (*Anno Domini,* Latin for "in the year of our Lord"). When religious leaders from other world religions passed away, the timeline never changed for them or acknowledged them. However, the world caught on and decided to use B.C.E. (Before Common Era) and C.E. (Common Era), trying to eradicate the truth of God's fingerprint on humanity.

The minute we mention Jesus in conversation, the fight is on. The devil knew this truth, so he created many religions to make it difficult and confusing for anyone to desire the only true and living God. We must take the kingdom of God by force and stand for Jesus, even in life-or-death situations. Jesus has been the most talked about, the most controversial, the most fought over individual of all human history, not to mention the wars for Israel and Jerusalem, the "City of the Great King." Modern Israel became a nation on May 14, 1948 after 2,534 years of nonexistence since the days of Nebuchadnezzar. Israel took control of Jerusalem in 1967, and they have been attacked ever since. These two events are prophetic in our history; they are the super signs Jesus talked about, connecting the fig tree to His eminent return to earth in invisible form during the Rapture (see 1 Cor. 15:52; 1 Thess. 4:16, 17).

EXAMINE YOURSELF

The attitude, "Stop being so spiritual and religious," is the trademark and justification of carnal and counterfeit Christians, when in fact they need to examine themselves and stop eating the Holy Communion every month at church in an unworthy manner. Otherwise the judgment of death or sickness will fall on them, especially if they are not ignorant of the sinfulness of their actions.

> *Therefore whoever eats this bread or drinks this cup of the Lord in an unworthy manner will be guilty of the body and blood of the Lord. But let a man examine himself, and so let him eat of the bread and drink of the cup. For he who eats and drinks in an unworthy manner eats and drinks judgment to himself, not discerning the Lord's body. For this reason many are weak and sick among you, and many sleep. For if we would judge ourselves, we would not be judged. But when we are judged, we are chastened by the Lord, that we may not be condemned with the world*
> (1 Corinthians 11:27-32 NKJV).

Jesus is watching every step we walk on earth, mindful to what will become of us in the future. We have to pray to make sure we get on the ball. Prayer is very important if we want our loved ones to be led to salvation. We must also pray for those who are "playing church" while walking with the knowledge of who Christ is, but we must also stay away from them so that satan is not able to use them for our ill will. We Christians must get it together so we can erect the Kingdom of Christ for the glory of God the Father and His Holy Spirit.

As a holy people, we must stand against the devil and his legions, forbidding ourselves from letting our guard down for a moment. No matter where we are or where we go, we have to stand and fight for what is right in the sight of the Lord at all times as best we know how. Prayer is a very important weapon and will change all of our circumstances if we are consistent. As a righteous community of believers, we have to come against complacency and mediocrity. The Lord desires for us to prosper and be in health, to build churches and community outreach centers, to provide food, water, and medical supplies to all in need. In His eyes, it doesn't matter if people are our enemies or loved ones; we must do for all as we do for our own. *"But if any provide not for his own, and specially for those of his own house, he hath denied the faith, and is worse than an infidel"* (1 Tim. 5:8). We are a world community of the human race—one blood, one Lord, one baptism—a global family of born-again believers.

WALK IN THE SPIRIT SO YOU MAY STAND

As you well know, we must always walk in the spirit to make sure we always have the upper hand to stand against temptation and the wiles of the enemy. It is not a walk in a park, but it is possible. We have a helper (who is the Holy

Ghost) that will support us and pick us up when we fall down. As a man or woman of God, we have been given the tools to stand when it is required of us. One of the great tools given by the apostle Paul under the inspiration of the Spirit of God to us is in Romans 8, it reads:

> *There is therefore now no condemnation to those who are in Christ Jesus, who do not walk according to the flesh, but according to the Spirit. For the law of the Spirit of life in Christ Jesus has made me free from the law of sin and death. For what the law could not do in that it was weak through the flesh, God did by sending His own Son in the likeness of sinful flesh, on account of sin: He condemned sin in the flesh, that the righteous requirement of the law might be fulfilled in us who do not walk according to the flesh but according to the Spirit. For those who live according to the flesh set their minds on the things of the flesh, but those who live according to the Spirit, the things of the Spirit. For to be carnally minded is death, but to be spiritually minded is life and peace. Because the carnal mind is enmity against God for it is not subject to the law of God, nor indeed can be. So then, those who are in the flesh cannot please God. But you are not in the flesh but in the Spirit, if indeed the Spirit of God dwells in you. Now if anyone does not have the Spirit of Christ, he is not His. And if Christ is in you, the body is dead because of sin, but the Spirit is life because of righteousness. But if the Spirit of Him who raised Jesus from the dead dwells in you, He who raised*

*Christ from the dead will also give life to your
mortal bodies through His Spirit who dwells in
you. Therefore, brethren, we are debtors—not to
the flesh, to live according to the flesh. For if you
live according to the flesh you will die but if by the
Spirit you put to death the deeds of the body, you
will live* (Romans 8:1-13 NASB).

SIGNS OF THE END OF THE AGE

One of the reasons why, in these last days, we must
stand up for Christ is because the end is very, very near.
Early one morning, in 2003, the Holy Spirit woke me up
at 7:17 A.M. and spoke to me, revealing specifically and
clearly that Revelation 18 is the prophecy toward America,
political Babylon, when the Church is gone. There are two
Babylons in the Bible, political and religious. I believe we
are political Babylon.

In Revelation 18:4, it says, *"Come up out of her my
people...,"* signifying the Rapture (the Latin is *Rapiomore*;
the Greek is *Harpazo*). Therefore, we will not take part of
the Tribulation or the Great Tribulation. The first Tribulation is the "Wrath of the Lamb" (see Rev. 6:16) and
the second, the Great Tribulation, is the "Wrath of God"
(see Rev. 14:10). The Lord will not allow His Bride to go
through so much devastation and pandemonium, just like
any husband who loves his wife will not allow such horror
to come upon her. Here are several references proving the
"Bride of Christ" will not go through this horrific episode:

*The voice of my beloved! Behold, He comes
Leaping upon the mountains, Skipping upon the*

hills. My beloved is like a gazelle or a young stag. Behold, he stands behind our wall; **He is looking through the windows** *(Heaven), Gazing through the lattice. My beloved spoke, and said to me:* **"Rise up, my love, my fair one, and come away** *(Come up here!). For lo, the winter is past, the rain is over and gone. The flowers appear on the earth; the time of singing has come, and the voice of the turtledove is heard in our land. The fig tree (Israel) puts forth her green figs, and the vines with the tender grapes give a good smell.* **Rise up, my love, my fair one, and come away** [Rapture: Come up here] (Song of Solomon 2:8-13 NKJV).

But take heed to yourselves; lest your hearts be weighed down with carousing, drunkenness, and cares of this life, and that Day come on you unexpectedly. For it will come as a snare on all those who dwell on the face of the whole earth. **Watch therefore, and pray always that you may be counted worthy to escape all these things that will come to pass, and to stand before the Son of Man** (Luke 21:34-36 NKJV).

Behold, I tell you a mystery: We shall not all sleep, but we shall all be changed—in a moment, in the twinkling of an eye, at the last trumpet. For **the trumpet will sound, and the dead will be raised incorruptible, and we shall be changed.** *For this corruptible must put on incorruption, and this mortal must put on immortality. So when* *this corruptible has put on incorruption, and this mortal has put on immortality, then shall be brought to pass the saying that is written: "Death is swallowed up in victory." "O Death, where is your sting? O Hades, where is your victory?"* (1 Corinthians 15:51-55 NKJV)

For this we say to you by the word of the Lord, that we who are alive and remain until the coming of the Lord will by no means precede those who are asleep. **For the Lord Himself will descend from heaven with a shout,** *with the voice of an archangel, and with the trumpet of God. And the dead in Christ will rise first.* **Then we who are alive and remain shall be caught up together with them in the clouds to meet the Lord in the air.** *And thus we shall always be with the Lord. Therefore comfort one another with these words* (1 Thessalonians 4:15-18 NKJV).

Looking for **the blessed hope and glorious appearing of our great God and Savior Jesus Christ,** *who gave Himself for us, that He might redeem us from every lawless deed and purify for Himself His own special people, zealous for good works* (Titus 2:13-14 NKJV).

Because you have kept My command to persevere, I also will keep you from the hour of trial, which shall come upon the whole world, *to test those who dwell on the earth* (Revelation 3:10 NKJV).

And I heard another voice from heaven saying,
**"Come out of her, my people, lest you share in
her sins, and lest you receive of her plagues**
(Revelation 18:4 NKJV).

As we mull over these Holy promises of God, let's
remember Noah. The King of the universe placed him in
the ark and shut the door, saving him from the outside
destruction where there was no life (see Gen. 7). The Lord
also guided Lot and his two daughters out of Sodom and
Gomorrah before He destroyed the cities with fire and
brimstone, which his wife, Ado, died for looking back (see
Gen. 19:26). Before God decided to destroy Nineveh, He
sent a prophet to warn them, giving them an opportunity to
come to repentance and be saved (see Jonah 1:1). Moreover,
150 years later, God explained the destruction of Nineveh
for returning to their sins (see Nah. 1-3). Although they
went back to their vomit (sin), if they would have stayed
in a righteous state, God would have kept His part of the
deal. Numerous occasions of God's *agape* love poured over
the timeline of history prove His true attributes as a loving
Father of all creation.

As I have pointed out earlier, we must get ready for
Jesus' prominent return. There are 10,385 passages in the
Bible on eschatology (the study of the end times) alone; 27
percent of the Bible is about the study of last things and the
end of the age as we know it. Out of that amount, there are
1,000 prophecies in His Word, of which 500 have come to
pass. The rest will be fulfilled as soon as we go home to
be with the Lord. America and the rest of the world are so
clueless and are in such darkness, while satan and his evil
hordes are murdering, slaying, abusing, human trafficking,

drugging, and killing our families, friends, people around the world, and even Christians! As long as there is breath in my body, my wife and I will do *all* that we can in the mighty name of Jesus to lead hundreds of millions to our Lord and Savior Jesus the Christ! Watch and pray!

I pray that we will come together, love each other as we should, and lead people to the Savior of the world the best we know how. Let us rise up together. No longer will we be labeled counterfeit Christians; let's not be artificial, but faithful and true to God and one another. Follow me as I follow Christ, and let's rise up together!

In Jesus' name, rise up, His pastors! Rise up, His evangelists! Rise up, His prophets! Rise up, His teachers! Rise up, His apostles! Rise up, His bishops, deacons, ministers, and the rest of the congregational members! Let's take dominion and the Kingdom by force!

PRAYER

I thank you Father that you have called me to be your minister in these last days. You have given me so much. I feel like I have no way to repay you for all your goodness you have shown me, except by giving you my entire life. Lord, right now I ask you to raise me up in these last-days, according to your will, and your will alone, so I may be used mightily and lead many souls to salvation. Standing up for you and being truly genuine before Your eyes will be my task. I confess I will not be known as Counterfeit Christian, but a Christian that will stand for You no matter what obstacle I face. You are heart of my heart, soul of my soul, you mean everything to me Lord. I need you continuously! I pray that I never put anyone above You. Thank you in advance for what you are going to accomplish in my life. In Jesus' name, Amen.

Conclusion

The chapters you read were steps for new believers and the well-seasoned alike. If you follow the pattern of the chapters, it all comes together so you will know how to guard your heart and spirit, empowering you to be able to go through the valley of brokenness. Once you reach that level, the fear of the Lord can reign in your heart. When you fear the Lord, the Lord's wisdom becomes part of your nature, and then you can ask the Lord, "Who do You say that I am?" In the beginning of your salvation experience, you went to the cross and became more than a conqueror in the eyes of the Lord so that you can worship the only true living God in spirit and in truth. This enables you to fight the world's lust in order to know your true purpose. Afterward, the living water will give you the cogency to be authentic, so when Jesus asks you, "Who here is on my side?" you can respond with boldness and confidence as God allows the real Christian to stand up for Him!

ALL IS GOING TO BE WELL

This is a word from glory to the nations of the earth. Hallelujah to the Lamb of God, who took away the sins of the world! I have so much hope for you and your entire family; it burns within my members. I declare to you right now that your children and loved ones and those for whom you are praying for salvation will come back home and come back to the Spirit, giving their lives to Christ. And you will give God glory because they will minister the Word of God to the lost in the end days; some will be saved and preach in the time of the tribulation, leading many to salvation! Nevertheless, they will receive their crown of Life! Wait for it. It will come to pass!

PROPHETIC WORD FOR THE NATION

The Lord says, *"My Spirit will reign in the earth, no one will forget who I AM. I AM the Almighty and Everlasting. My voice will be known through-out every people, tongue, kindred, and nation. All things will submit to Me, from all places, all areas, all realms! America will come to turmoil, and you will see her no more after My Spirit brings revival for My children. I AM the Alpha and Omega, from Everlast-ing to Everlasting! No one will be able to hide from My presence; no one will escape from My blessings. The same will fall on those who are disobedient to Me; they will not be able to escape My presence, they will not be able to escape My judgment. Get prepared for my Coming. I AM building up My people who are called by My name and all those who answered the*

Call. My anointing and those who are anointed will begin the revival for My Coming."
—Apostle Luis Lopez

Final Thoughts
From the Author

The Counterfeit Christian has been a blessing, an honor, and a privilege to write. I thank God with all of my being for anointing me and for opening this door for me to take part in helping to prepare the Body of Christ for the return of Jesus Christ.

It has been a very challenging and awesome experience writing to you. You mean so much to me. I worked meticulously, writing for many hours a day to make sure that what is written would be a huge blessing to you as you read this right beside your Bible. The enemy has tried so hard to make sure this book did not make it into the hands of my publisher. Guess what? He lost again! Praise God!

Only by the grace of God and His anointing I am able to inscribe what He has put in my heart on paper. My prayer and hope is that you were left with just a little more knowledge, wisdom, and determination to walk in peace and humility.

As you well know, I have gone through so much in my life. And there are many who would make what I went through very simplistic, but my focus is making sure your walk with Christ will not be hindered nor your prayer life sabotaged. Prayer is the weapon and life support of the believer.

In conclusion, allow yourself to seal these pages with new thoughts, a right spirit, and holy concepts, taking what God has already engineered into the pages of your own life. Never to travel on the path of becoming a counterfeit Christian, but be a person who is chasing after God. Always be aware of the enemy so that your focus can be consistently clear and you can know your true purpose here on earth. Filled with the love, power, compassion, mercy, and grace of the Holy Spirit, channel these things through yourself to others to be a blessing. God will always love you, and so will I, until the end of the age. May the Lord God truly bless you at all times and forevermore.

Appendix A

Prayer of Salvation

Father, I am a sinner, and I ask You to forgive me of my sins. Cleanse me with Your blood and wash me from all unrighteousness. I believe that Jesus died on the cross for my sins, and on the third day, You raised Him from the dead. Father, I ask You to fill me with Your Holy Spirit right now and write my name in the Lamb's Book of Life. I give my entire life to You from this day onward. In Jesus' name I pray, amen.

If you confess with your mouth the Lord Jesus and believe in your heart that God has raised Him from the dead, you will be saved. For with the heart one believes unto righteousness, and with the mouth confession is made unto salvation (Romans 10:9-10 NKJV).

About Luis Lopez

Ordained as an apostle, Luis Lopez was born in Brooklyn, New York. He was brought up in the house of God. While he was still young, his grandmother taught him about Jesus Christ and how He would save people and change their lives significantly. In the late 1980s, Luis moved from Brooklyn, New York, to Rochester, New York, where he became a born-again Christian at the age of 15. After serving the Lord for a while, he backslid for a season and experienced different influences in his life. Yet, the Holy Spirit kept him from the things of the world and never released him from His sight. He came back to the Lord afresh and is still serving the Lord faithfully, 'til this day.

Apostles, prophets, pastors, and saints of the Lord speak greatly of Apostle Luis and his ministry. The moving of the Holy Spirit is evident in his life when he speaks. In fact, when Luis speaks, it is apparent that he has a teaching anointing, as the Spirit of the Lord leads him. He loves the Lord with all of his heart, soul, mind, and strength and yearns to win souls for the Kingdom of God. Luis has been married to Michelle Lopez since May of 2002. They have four children. He and his wife are the founders and chief overseers of Luis Lopez International Ministries, Kingdom Fire International Church, and International Connection of Apostles & Prophets.

He is an honest and dedicated man of God. His calling is specifically in the area of revelatory teaching, dreams, and visions, miracles, signs, and wonders; and he operates in the five-fold ministry. He has been mandated and sent by the Lord Jesus to prepare the Body of Christ for the second advent of Christ, in parallel to how God used John the Baptizer to prepare His people of the first coming. Thus shall it be again. He was called and ordained as the Lord's apostle from his mother's womb.

In 2003, Jesus appeared to him in a vision and took him up in the spirit to the third Heaven, where he saw Christ seated on His Throne. Since this vision in 2003, he has been intensely receiving dreams, visions, and revelations. He has also received prophetic and audible dreams, visions, and divine revelation of the Word, the tribulation period, and the end of the age.

Contact:

Luis Lopez International Ministries
PO Box 31948
Rochester, NY 14603
Office: 1-800-420-7690
Email: contactus@luislopezministries.com
Church Email: kingdomfirechurch@yahoo.com
Website: www.luislopezministries.com

In the right hands, This Book will Change Lives!

Most of the people who need this message will not be looking for this book. To change their lives, you need to put a copy of this book in their hands.

> *But others (seeds) fell into good ground, and brought forth fruit, some a hundred-fold, some sixty-fold, some thirty-fold* (Matthew 13:8).

Our ministry is constantly seeking methods to find the good ground, the people who need this anointed message to change their lives. Will you help us reach these people?

> *Remember this—a farmer who plants only a few seeds will get a small crop. But the one who plants generously will get a generous crop* (2 Corinthians 9:6).

EXTEND THIS MINISTRY BY SOWING
3 BOOKS, 5 BOOKS, 10 BOOKS, OR MORE TODAY,
AND BECOME A LIFE CHANGER!

Thank you,

Don Nori Sr., Founder
Destiny Image
Since 1982